# THE TURBULENT ERA:

## Riot & Disorder in Jacksonian America

MICHAEL FELDBERG
*Boston University*

OXFORD UNIVERSITY PRESS
New York          1980          Oxford

973.6
Fe

Library of Congress Cataloging in Publication Data

Feldberg, Michael.
    The turbulent era.

    Bibliography: p.
    Includes index.
    1. Riots—United States—History—19th century.
2. Philadelphia—Riots, 1844. 3. Violence—United
States—History—19th century. I. Title.
HV6477.F44    301.6'332'0973    79-17705
ISBN 0-19-502677-2
ISBN 0-19-502678-0 pbk.

Printed in the United States of America

# Preface

This is a book about riots: what they were like in Jacksonian America, why they were so prevalent during that era, and how they have changed since that time. A riot is an incident in which dozens, hundreds, or thousands of persons gather—either with or without prior planning—and use violence to injure or intimidate their victims. Violence is the infliction of pain, injury, or damage to persons or property. Rioting in the 1830s, 1840s, and 1850s usually involved two groups of citizens battling each other, but they also could consist of groups attacking isolated individuals or groups confronting the official forces of order. Most of the examples of rioting offered in this book are set in Philadelphia, not because William Penn's "City of Brotherly Love" was more subject to collective violence than, say, New York or Boston, but because my own research has made me most familiar with the history of Jacksonian Philadelphia.

My use of the term "Jacksonian" in this volume is quite loose. Most often, the term is used to delineate a time period: the 1830s and 1840s. Similarly, the term "Jacksonians" usually means Americans who lived through that period, although it sometimes refers to the supporters of President Andrew Jackson. Some of the events and phenomena discussed in the volume deal also with the 1850s, a period designated by most historians as the "antebellum period." I have chosen to refer to the 1830s, 1840s, and 1850s as a whole as the Jacksonian era or the pre-Civil War period.

Since this volume is written for a general audience, I have kept footnoting to a minimum. The bibliographical essay at the conclusion of the text will indicate the major works from which I have drawn, and to which the reader with further interest in the history of collective violence should go. Persons already familiar with the historiography of Jacksonian rioting will recognize my debt to other scholars, but I would like to acknowledge my reliance on the careful scholarship of Richard Maxwell Brown, David Grimsted, David Montgomery, Leonard L. Richards, and Sam Bass Warner, Jr.

A number of persons deserve special thanks. David Reimers and Thomas Bender, consulting editors for this volume, honored me by suggesting that I undertake this project. Nancy Lane of Oxford University Press has extended courtesy, assistance, and patience in the project's course of development. My loyal friends Joseph Boskin, Edward Berger, and Howard Cohen read, criticized, and improved the manuscript. Deborah F. Galiga, Joyce Davis, and Lisa Boodman tirelessly labored over the typing of several drafts. My wife Ruth contributed her editorial skills, her encouragement, and her trust. To her, to Gabriel, and to Nyssa, Pamela, Sara, and Tabitha, many thanks for the joy and the love that has sustained my work.

M. F.

*Cambridge, Massachusetts*
*October 1979*

# Contents

# The Turbulent Era

# Introduction

Americans who remember the urban unrest of the 1960s can readily identify with the crisis of violence that gripped Jacksonian American cities. The 1830s, 1840s, and 1850s produced a constant stream of riots reminiscent of the "long hot summers" of the not-too-distant past. Jacksonian cities were torn by fighting between immigrants and native-born Americans, abolitionists and anti-abolitionists, free blacks and racist whites, volunteer firefighters and street gangs, Mormons and "Gentiles," even rival factions of Whigs and Democrats. And, like the 1960s, Jacksonian collective violence resulted in greatly enlarged and strengthened police forces better able to repress riots and disorders—either with or without death or injury to the rioters.

Yet there are some notable differences between the upheavals of the pre-Civil War decades and those of the 1960s. Compared with the death and devastation in Watts, Newark, or Detroit, Jacksonian rioting seems rather tame. Whereas a few major confrontations in the 1840s and 1850s took the lives of at least a dozen persons, deaths in Jacksonian rioting were a relatively rare occurrence. Certainly the property damage to Washington, D.C., after the assassination of Martin Luther King, Jr., or to Harlem during the New York Blackout of 1977, was unequaled by even the most destructive pre-Civil War violence.

In its own way, however, urban rioting posed for Jacksonian society a social and political crisis seemingly equal to that of the 1960s' era of protest. To some contemporaries, violence in the 1830s and 1840s portended the possible destruction of American civilization. The upper-class Philadelphian, Sidney George Fisher, for example, predicted that the United States was "destined to be destroyed by the eruption of the dark masses of ignorance and brutality which lie beneath it, like the fires of a volcano."[1] As sober an analyst as Abraham Lincoln warned in 1837 that

> . . . there is even now something of an ill omen amongst us. I mean the increasing disregard for law which pervades the country —the growing disposition to substitute the wild and furious passions in lieu of the sober judgment of the courts, and the worse than savage mobs for the executive ministers of justice. This disposition is awfully fearful in any community; and that it now exists in ours, though grating to our feelings to admit it, would be a violation of truth and an insult to our intelligence to deny. Accounts of outrages committed by mobs form the every-day news of the times. They have pervaded the country from New England to Louisiana; they are neither peculiar to the eternal snows of the former nor the burning suns of the latter; they are not the creatures of climate, neither are they confined to the slaveholding

---

1. Sidney George Fisher, *A Philadelphia Perspective: The Diary of Sidney George Fisher, Covering the Years 1834-1871,* N. B. Wainwright, ed. (Philadelphia, 1967), p. 169.

or the non-slaveholding states. Alike they spring up among the pleasure-hunting master of Southern slaves, and the order-loving citizens of the land of steady habits. Whatever their causes be, it is common to the whole country.[2]

Lincoln was not exaggerating the dimensions of the crisis. Historian Richard Maxwell Brown has counted thirty-five major riots in Baltimore, Philadelphia, New York, and Boston during the three decades from 1830 to 1860. Historian John C. Schneider found that "at least seventy percent of American cities with a population of twenty thousand or more by 1850 experienced some degree of major disorder in the 1830–1865 period."[3] The abolitionist movement, which kept its own count of anti-abolition and racially motivated mobs, reported no less than 209 such incidents for the 1830s and 1840s alone. With good reason Lincoln lamented that rioting had become "the everyday news of the times."[4]

Despite the anxiety that collective violence was able to create in contemporaries, the Jacksonian era was far from the most bloody in the nation's history. That distinction belongs to the Civil War era, starting with the mid-1850s guerrilla wars in Kansas and ending with the Ku Klux Klan violence of Southern Reconstruction during the 1860s and 1870s. Jacksonian violence was also vastly overshadowed by the mass slaughter of the Plains Indians in the years after 1870, and by the labor and industrial violence of the late nineteenth and early twentieth centuries. Nonetheless, the 1830s, 1840s, and 1850s were probably marked by a higher *frequency* and variety of urban

2. T. Harry Williams, ed., *Abraham Lincoln: Selected Speeches, Messages and Letters* (New York, 1957), p. 7.

3. John C. Schneider, "Mob Violence and Public Order in the American City" (Ph. D. dissertation, University of Minnesota, 1971). Quoted in Richard Maxwell Brown, *Strain of Violence: Historical Studies of American Violence and Vigilantism* (New York, 1975), p. 3.

4. Williams, p. 14.

collective violence and disorder among private groups than was any equivalent period of time in the nation's past. In the 1830s and 1840s particularly, there seem to have been few if any causes, issues, disagreements, or rivalries that could not incite a riot, and few social groups or political factions that would not resort to violence to further their aims or to express their emotions. Baltimore newspaper editor Hezekiah Niles despaired of this popular tendency of Americans to "take the law into their own hands," spreading a "spirit of riot . . . in every quarter."[5]

The historical significance of rioting in a given period should not be measured solely by its frequency or intensity. Collective violence should be judged in its broader social and political contexts as well; it must be seen as one of several forms of interaction that can occur among groups, or between groups and their government. We must look at the functions Jacksonian rioting served, the kinds of groups that employed it, and the success of those groups in using violence to attain their goals. In the Jacksonian context, collective violence was one means by which various groups attempted to control competition among themselves, or by which they responded to changes in their relative status, power, wealth, or political influence.

My examination of Jacksonian collective violence begins with a close look at the Philadelphia Native American Riots of 1844, and then shifts to an analysis of the major categories of pre-Civil War collective violence: anti-immigrant, religious, anti-abolitionist, anti-black, and other forms of what I have called *political* collective violence. The inquiry then proceeds to the phenomenon of expressive and recreational riots: gang fights, firemen's fights, election riots, community solidarity riots, labor and strike violence, and vigilante movements. As these explorations will reveal, Jacksonian collective violence stemmed

5. Quoted in Leonard L. Richards, *"Gentlemen of Property and Standing": Anti-Abolition Mobs in Jacksonian America* (New York, 1970), p. 9.

from a number of sources: the racial and ethnic tensions of the period; the era's ideological climate; the inability of political systems and legal institutions to resolve group conflict by peaceable means; rapid urbanization and population changes; and economic and technological innovation. What distinguishes Jacksonian rioting from collective violence in other periods of American history is not its sources, however, but the frequency of its occurrence, its effectiveness, and the relative inability of public authorities to control or suppress it. Yet the very success achieved by private groups through rioting called forth forces that, by the 1850s, would change the balance of power between rioters and local peacekeeping officials and impose professional police systems on American cities. The epidemic of collective violence in Jacksonian cities ultimately undermined the American public's traditional resistance to the creation of effective urban police forces. By the time of the Civil War, most of the nation's important cities had established recognizably modern police departments. While urban rioting by no means disappeared after the Civil War, by the 1870s, outside of the Reconstruction South, groups that employed violence for their own personal or political ends almost always found themselves confronting official forces of order rather than rival private groups. The creation of urban police departments became the most enduring legacy of Jacksonian collective violence.

The great Philadelphia Native American Riots of 1844 were certainly among the most dramatic and violent episodes in pre-Civil War American history. In both their Kensington and Southwark phases, they present a capsule portrait of the sources, uses, and consequences of Jacksonian collective violence. Although they grew out of cultural and religious conflict between Philadelphia's Protestant nativists and Irish Catholic immigrants, the riots were the immediate result of a political controversy over the use of the Bible in the Philadelphia public schools. The fighting also reflected the social and political disorganization of Philadelphia and the weakness of its peacekeeping system. On May fourth through sixth, nativists and immigrants confronted each other directly in Kensington, an industrial suburb on the northern boundary of Philadelphia proper. In early July, angry nativists confronted state militia troops in Southwark, a working-class neighborhood on the city's southern edge, and the soldiers narrowly defeated their civilian rivals in a bitter battle fought with rifles and cannons. Above all, the two phases of the Philadelphia Native American Riots of 1844 illustrate the ease with which private groups in Jacksonian America employed collective violence as a tool for conducting social conflict and expressing political protest. The riots also reveal the difficulties public authorities faced when they tried to control group violence in the nation's rapidly changing cities.

# 1. The Philadelphia Native American Riots of 1844:

## The Kensington Phase

By February 1844, Louisa Bedford had finally run out of patience. She was having a difficult enough time teaching elementary school in Kensington, a working-class suburb just north of Philadelphia. Now her job was made even more trying because of hard feelings between the parents of both her immigrant Irish Catholic students and her native-born Protestant students. The problem revolved around the use of the Bible as a reading book in the Philadelphia county public schools. Two years earlier, in 1842, the Philadelphia County Board of School Controllers had ordered that the King James, or Protestant, version of Holy Scripture be used as a basic reading text in all Philadelphia public-school classes. Upon hearing this, the Catholic Bishop of Philadelphia, the Reverend Francis Patrick Kenrick, asked that Catholic children be allowed to read the Douay, or authorized

Catholic, version of Scripture, and that Catholic teachers not be compelled to read from the King James during reading exercises. The controllers denied Kenrick's request.

During the 1840s many American Protestants feared Catholicism because it seemed alien and anti-democratic. Protestants believed that the pope and his priests controlled the minds of their followers, and that the papacy was dedicated to overthrowing the American way of life. Because of this widely held prejudice, the Philadelphia School Controllers were afraid to grant equal status to the Douay Bible by allowing it in the schools. They feared that angry Protestant voters would turn them out of office at the next election, and no controller wanted to volunteer for political extinction. Yet to ease Bishop Kenrick's objections to an obvious injustice, the Board of School Controllers saw fit to offer a compromise solution: Catholic children could leave their classrooms while Bible-reading exercises were conducted, but the Douay version was still not to be admitted into the schools.

This compromise pleased almost no one. Catholics believed that the plan ignored their bishop's plea for justice and equality; evangelical Protestants felt that Catholic children should be compelled to read the King James version as an antidote to their "priestly dictated" and "popish" beliefs. The solution also failed to please teachers like Louisa Bedford, who could not tolerate the disruption caused by her Catholic students waiting noisily outside her door until the Bible-reading session was over. To remedy this situation, Bedford took actions which, in a short time, led to the great Philadelphia riots of 1844.

Louisa Bedford was a Protestant, although not a militant evangelical. Seriously committed to teaching the working-class children of Kensington to read and write, she resented the chaos caused by the controllers' policy. Thus when School Controller and Irish Catholic politician Hugh Clark was making his weekly tour of Kensington's public schools, Bedford asked Clark if she could have a word with him. She explained her unhappiness to the politically astute Clark who, one suspects, was waiting for just such a moment. Clark then sympathetically offered an alternative to sending Catholic students out of her room: She could suspend *all* Bible reading in her class until such time as the School Controllers devised a better method for excusing Catholic students from the exercise. Clark volunteered to assume responsibility should she decide to follow this course. Bedford chose to accept Clark's offer and told her students that, for the time being, they would not have to do their Bible reading. Much to her relief, she turned to teaching other subjects.

While Louisa Bedford's discomfort was eased, severe problems for Hugh Clark and Philadelphia's Irish-Catholic community were just beginning. Word of Clark's decision to "kick the Bible out of the schools," as his enemies inaccurately described it, spread like wildfire throughout the city. Evangelical Protestants, most of them native-born Americans and the remainder immigrant Irish Protestants, had been organizing in Philadelphia for nearly a decade. The evangelicals were alarmed by what they believed to be the growing political and religious influence of Catholics, particularly Irish Catholic immigrants. Nativists, a name given to those who openly opposed all "alien" elements such as Catholics, immigrants, Mormons, and others who did not conform to the dominant white Protestant religious and cultural values of the era, had especially feared the political activism of the Irish Catholic clergy. Three years earlier, New York Bishop John Hughes had supported Catholic candidates for public office because the city's school board had refused to excuse Catholics from paying their school taxes. Hughes argued that Catholics should not be forced to support schools that were teaching Catholic students that the pope was "Antichrist" and that the Church of Rome was "The Whore of Babylon." Now Bishop Kenrick and Irish politicians like Hugh Clark were trying to meddle with Philadelphia's public schools. Perhaps, people believed, these Catholic efforts were nothing less than a dastardly plot to overthrow the public schools or turn them into centers for converting Protestant children.

To counter this threat to American religious, educational, and political institutions, Philadelphia's evangelicals organized a cluster of religiously oriented "reform" organizations: the American Protestant Association, which was a coalition of the city's Baptist, Methodist, and

Presbyterian ministers who lectured on the "evils" and "dangers" of Roman Catholic "superstition"; the Sabbatarian movement, which hoped to promote Protestant church attendance by suppressing Sunday amusements and diversions such as picnics, fairs, train travel, sporting events (especially boxing matches and horse races), gambling, Sunday mail deliveries, and the serving of alcohol in public places; and the colportage movement, which tried to place a free King James Bible in the hand of anyone who promised to read it.

Most important, Protestants concerned with the increasing influence of Catholics and immigrants in American life joined a new political movement known as the American Republican party, which had branches in Philadelphia, New York, Boston, Baltimore, and New Orleans. The American Republicans held rallies and ran candidates to oppose the influence of immigrants in local politics. While they did not call for a halt to foreign immigration, they stood on a three-plank platform that demanded (1) an extension to twenty-one years of the waiting period for naturalization (that is, the granting of citizenship and the right to vote); (2) the election of none but native-born Americans to public office; and (3) the rejection of "foreign interference" in the social, political, and religious institutions of the country, especially the public schools. As one Philadelphia nativist put it:

> The day must come, and, we fear, is not too far distant, when most of our offices will be held by foreigners—men who have no sympathy with the spirit of our institutions, who have done aught to secure the blessings they enjoy, and instead of governing ourselves, we shall be governed by men, many of whom, but a few short years previously, scarcely knew of our existence.[1]

For the most part, American Republican leadership in Philadelphia was composed of "middling" and "respectable" men: lawyers, doctors,

---

1. Quoted in Michael Feldberg, *The Philadelphia Riots of 1844: A Study of Ethnic Conflict* (Westport, Conn., 1975), p. 60.

clergymen, newspaper editors, shopkeepers, craftsmen, printers, barbers, dentists, and teachers. These individuals were neither numbered in the ranks of the city's traditional upper classes—wealthy merchants, bankers, manufacturers, and gentlemen farmers—nor drawn from the ranks of the struggling poor. Rather, these American Republicans had formerly provided the bulk of middle-class voters for the Whig and Democratic parties. With their wives they filled the pews of Philadelphia's Methodist, Baptist, and Presbyterian churches. By their own description they saw themselves as the "bone and sinew" of society, the hard-working silent majority who, while never independently wealthy and secure like the upper classes, would never allow themselves to fall to the level of the impoverished or degenerate immigrants.

Because they saw themselves as the nation's only "real" Americans, nativists could not stand to see their public schools, or the political system in general, "captured" by persons who spoke with a foreign accent—especially an Irish brogue. The social isolation of America's Irish immigrants and their continued loyalty to their native land particularly worried American nativists. They believed that the typical Irish immigrant would never become a loyal American citizen, freed of his allegiance to Ireland or to the Roman Catholic Church. They did not realize that the experiences of Irish Catholic immigrants with English-speaking Protestants had convinced the Irish to cling to their religion and to their nationalism.

For almost two centuries before their arrival in Jacksonian America, Irish Catholics had been fighting against their Protestant English rulers for the right to political independence and religious liberty. Even after transplanting themselves in American soil, Irish immigrants lost little dedication to the cause of Irish freedom. Catholic priests who migrated with their flocks kept alive the memory of injustices inflicted by the Protestant ruling class on Ireland's Catholic majority: military occupation; government by the English Parliament rather than by Irish home rule; the suspension of the right of Irish children to receive a Catholic education. Thus for the immigrant Irish, the cause of a free Ireland and the cause of the Irish Catholic Church were inseparable.

To maintain their solidarity, to resist integration into a Protestant-dominated society such as the one they had fled, the American Irish tended to cluster in self-imposed ghettos, to socialize in their own taverns, to attend mass in their own parish churches, and to meet in their own political and nationalist clubs. Such self-inflicted isolation upset Protestant American nativists, but the apparent political control that the Irish-born Catholic clergy seemed to exercise over their immigrant followers appeared to bother them even more. Nativists convinced one another that the American Irish voted overwhelmingly for the Democratic party, not because the Jacksonian political platform or personal style appealed to the newcomers, but because corrupt Roman Catholic priests "dictated" voting orders from Rome to their sheeplike parishioners. Nativists believed that such bloc voting threatened to turn American elections into mindless displays of numerical strength rather than expressions of reasoned judgment on issues or candidates.

The American Republicans determined to fight the power of the Catholic Church in the nation's political life. Their own forefathers had fought to drive foreign tyranny from the nation's shores during the American Revolution, and the American Republicans of 1844 would not stand idly by while the Roman Catholic Church attempted to substitute a new foreign tyranny in its place. The nativists based their ideology on two foundations: George Washington's famous Farewell Address, which urged his countrymen to "Beware of Foreign Influence"; and the concept of "Eternal Vigilance," or the principle that Americans, because their example of successful republicanism posed a threat to the kings and hereditary rulers of Europe, had to be on constant guard against attempts to subvert the American government.

Philadelphia American Republicanism was closely allied with the most popular reform movement of the era, the temperance crusade. At its inception in the early 1800s, the American temperance movement was dedicated to persuading individuals to consume only moderate amounts of alcoholic beverages. In the 1840s, its national membership may have numbered over 100,000, and most of these members believed that all sales of drinking alcohol should be outlawed. Alcoholism had become closely associated with poverty, unemployment, crime, ill health, and broken families. Somewhat unfairly, it was also closely associated with urban immigrant communities: gin and rum with the Irish, beer with the Germans, and wine with the French and Italians. Since nativists considered immigrant groups, and especially the Irish, responsible for most of the nation's poverty, crime, and prostitution, their interest in temperance reflected their critical attitudes toward the life-styles of America's urban immigrant populations.

It was unfair of nativists and temperance advocates to equate alcohol consumption primarily with immigrants. The nation's upper classes were the chief consumers of good French wines, port, sherry, and Madeira. Many native Protestant workingmen were paid a portion of their wages in a daily allowance of rum, and nearly every workshop and factory employed young boys to run out frequently for buckets of beer. Drinking to excess was a universal problem that crossed ethnic and class boundaries. The vast quantities of alcohol consumed in Jacksonian America convinced many temperance advocates, nativist and non-nativist alike, that an individual's mere verbal pledge to drink moderately was not enough to keep him from abusing alcohol, and temperance crusaders increasingly switched from a voluntarist to a prohibitionist position. They argued that only by outlawing the sale of liquor could its evil effects be controlled.

The conversion of Philadelphia's temperance movement to a prohibitionist stance was tied in important ways to the American Republican and evangelical Protestant movements of the era. Closing bars and rum shops could have important social and political implications for immigrant communities. Taverns were one of the focal points in working-class Irish and German neighborhoods, and they often served as social and political centers. Their patrons did not usually welcome native Protestant—or even other ethnic—outsiders, and many a Philadelphia brawl was started when an unwitting stranger of the wrong ethnic background violated the sanctity of a German or Irish saloon. Particularly in Irish neighborhoods, taverns became symbols of Irish-Catholic separatism and Irish immigrant rejection of integration into wider American culture.

But nativists had political as well as cultural objections to the immigrants' fondness for alcoholic beverages. They argued that just as priests could control the consciences of immigrant Catholics through the religious doctrine of papal infallibility, so could tavern owners manipulate the political loyalties of immigrants by trading liquor for votes. Nativist temperance advocates feared an unholy alliance between Catholic priests and ambitious tavern-owning politicians that would maintain the immigrants' dependence on the Church and the bottle. The battle against liquor, then, was in part a battle to preserve American political freedom from Catholic-sponsored conspiracies.

One person's reform, though, is another person's oppression, especially when the targets of the reform movement saw nothing wrong in their style of life or religious values. Catholic and Irish community leaders believed strongly that the Constitution entitled community members to liberty of conscience in their religion, freedom of association in their social contacts, freedom of thought in their political beliefs, and freedom of choice in their use of alcohol. The Catholic Archdiocese of Philadelphia organized its own voluntary temperance societies, but it strongly opposed any attempt to legislate away the individual's right to indulge in alcohol. And while it urged its parishioners to attend mass on Sunday, the Archdiocese resisted efforts to suppress popular amusements on the Sabbath. Most important, Bishop Kenrick personally resented the efforts of Protestant activists to "save" Catholic children by forcing them to read the King James Bible in the public schools.

Unfortunately for Bishop Kenrick and the rest of Philadelphia's Catholics, the school Bible issue stirred intense hatred in the "City of Brother Love." The city's nativists chose (deliberately or otherwise) to interpret Kenrick's request to grant equality to the Douay Bible as a demand that the King James Bible be *removed* from the public schools. They claimed that the bishop was plotting to make the schools "Godless," a prelude to rendering Protestant students ripe for conversion to the "superstition" of Catholicism. And it may well be that, in his heart, Bishop Kenrick would have preferred to see no Bible read at all in the school than to see Catholic children being forced to read the King James version. He may even have had doubts about their reading the Douay at school with no priest to officiate over the reading. But the bishop had the political wisdom not to call for Bibleless schools in Philadelphia's heated evangelical atmosphere. Instead, he chose to ask only that the Douay version be admitted to the classroom or that Catholic children be excused during Bible reading, regardless of the difficulties that such a practice might cause. Yet nativists continued to believe that Kenrick was planning to make the schools Bibleless, irreligious, and a breeding ground for a Catholic conspiracy to capture the souls of America's Protestant youth.

Thus it is clear why Hugh Clark's suggestion to Louisa Bedford that she suspend Bible reading in her Kensington classroom caused such upheaval throughout Philadelphia. It was as if the bishop's alleged conspiracy had finally come out in the open. The first word of Clark's actions was carried by Henry Moore, a Methodist minister who burst into a prayer meeting at his Kensington church to inform the congregation that Clark had forced Miss Bedford against her will to "kick the Bible out of her classroom." Word spread rapidly throughout the city's nativist network, and Philadelphia's American Republican leaders and evangelical Protestant clergymen convened a series of mass rallies in

mid-March to protest Catholic attempts to "trample our free Protestant institutions in the dust." At one rally more than 3,000 protestors gathered to hear an American Republican spokesman remind
those who would "remove the Bible from the public schools" that,
"when we remember that our Pilgrim Fathers landed on Plymouth
Rock to establish the Protestant religion, free from persecution, we
must contend that this was and always will be a Protestant country."[2]

Their enthusiastic reception at the city-wide rallies encouraged the
American Republicans to carry their crusade right to the lair of the
beast, the very neighborhood that symbolized Irish Catholic solidarity
in Philadelphia: Third Ward, Kensington. The community was long
and widely recognized as immigrant Irish "turf." It was dominated by
Irish handloom weavers, dock laborers, teamsters, and other semi-
skilled workers who held little love for their native Protestant neighbors in adjoining wards. The neighborhood had been the scene of
several riots in recent years, including a series of attacks on railroad
construction workers trying to lay tracks down Front Street and some
violent attacks on nonunion weavers who were failing to honor a
strike by their fellow "brothers of the loom." Perhaps the most
notorious incident had occurred a few months earlier, when the striking weavers attacked and dispersed a sheriff's posse, beat the sheriff
soundly, and had to be quelled by the state militia troops. It was in this
neighborhood of militant and aggressive Irish immigrants that the
American Republicans chose to hold a rally on Friday afternoon, May 3,
1844, and invite the general public to attend.

That Friday meeting might well have been calculated to provoke a
fateful confrontation with Kensington's immigrant Irish. The American Republicans chose to hold their rally in a schoolyard at Second and
Master streets. When the American Republican spokesmen began
their speeches, they were heckled, booed, and pelted with rocks and
garbage by a crowd of several hundred, and eventually driven from the

2. Feldberg, p. 95.

speaker's platform they had erected earlier in the afternoon. Undaunted (and quite self-righteously), the party decided to reconvene the meeting in the schoolyard on Monday, May 6, and placarded the city with notices urging every American Republican loyalist to attend. This time a large crowd of 3,000 turned out. Around 3:00 P.M., while noted temperance lecturer and political nativist Lewis C. Levin was arousing the crowd's interest, a sudden rainstorm erupted and the crowd moved spontaneously in search of shelter toward the Nanny Goat Market.

Relocating the rally in the market proved catastrophic. The Nanny Goat Market was the hub of the Third Ward Irish community. An open-sided, block-long covered shed at Third and Master streets, the market house served as a shopping center, a meeting place, and a social center for local residents. When the noisy but peaceable nativists arrived, a group of thirty or so Irish locals was waiting there to greet them. One Irishman was heard to proclaim, "Keep the damned natives out of our market house; this ground don't belong to them, it's ours!" Lewis Levin tried to continue his speech from a vendor's stand but hecklers drowned him out. Pushing and shoving began, someone pulled a pistol, a rival dared him to shoot, he did, and panic erupted under the shed. The Irish residents fled to their nearby homes, but the nativists were trapped in the open-sided shed with few places to hide. A rain of gunfire poured down on them from surrounding buildings, most of it from the Hibernia Hose House, the headquarters of an Irish volunteer fire company. The first nativist killed in the shooting, nineteen-year-old George Schiffler, became a martyr to the cause. His name was soon immortalized when a nativist militia company, a volunteer fire company, and a fighting street gang each took his name as their own. In subsequent years the street gang known as the Schifflers would fight many battles with Philadelphia's Irish and Democratic street gangs and volunteer fire companies.

The initial advantage possessed by the Irish snipers was soon balanced by the arrival of approximately eighteen nativist reinforcements who brought rifles and shotguns with them. Protected by the fire of their own sharpshooters, nativists began making forays out of the Nanny Goat Market, breaking windows and doors of the houses from which gunfire had been coming and scattering the inhabitants. Several Irishmen were badly beaten and left for dead as others saw their homes and furniture wrecked by the furious nativists. Finally, after two hours of heavy fighting, Sheriff Morton McMichael and a posse of two hundred deputies arrived and the fighting subsided.

That night, when darkness descended on Kensington, nativists from every corner of Philadelphia found their way to the neighborhood around the Nanny Goat Market. Around 10:00 P.M. a crowd "collected in the vicinity of Franklin and Second streets," marched toward the Nanny Goat Market, and on the way "commenced breaking into the houses on both sides of the street, destroying the furniture, demolishing the windows, and rendering the houses completely uninhabitable." The crowd then arrived at the gates of the seminary of the Catholic Sisters of Charity and were threatening to burn it down when a group of Irish defenders "advanced from above and fired a volley of ball and buckshot into the crowd."[3] One nativist attacker died instantly, a second lingered for a month before dying of a chest wound, and several others were injured. On this note, Monday night's fighting in Kensington drew to a close.

Philadelphians awakened Tuesday morning, May 7, to find their city plastered with printed calls to a rally protesting the murder of George Schiffler. The message ended with the inflammatory words, "LET EVERY MAN COME PREPARED TO DEFEND HIMSELF." That morning, the nativist press was filled with militant cries for revenge. The daily *Native American* proclaimed:

> Another St. Bartholomew's day has begun in the streets of Philadelphia. The bloody hand of the Pope has stretched forth to our destruction. Now we call on our fellow-citizens, who regard free

3. Feldberg, p. 106.

institutions, whether they be native or adopted, to arm. Our liberties are to be fought for—let us not be slack in our preparation.[4]

By 3:30 P.M. that Tuesday afternoon, more than 3,000 persons had gathered behind Independence Hall to hear speeches condemning Kensington's Irish. Despite the fact that the call to the meeting had broadly implied that those attending should carry arms, neither Sheriff McMichael nor the commander of the state militia in Philadelphia, General George Cadwalader, had gathered his forces in anticipation of more fighting. Kensington's Irish, on the other hand, seemed better prepared for what was to come.

When the speeches were finished and the American Republicans called for the meeting to adjourn, a voice in the crowd shouted, "Adjourn to Kensington right now!" The crowd took up the call, marched in loose military fashion out of the meeting ground, and turned northward to Kensington. When they arrived in the neighborhood of Second and Master, the marchers found that many of Kensington's Irish had fled the neighborhood and taken their belongings with them. Other inhabitants simply waited at home with their loaded guns. This time, the nativist procession did not pause to convene a meeting and hear speeches, but immediately attacked the Hibernia Hose House. Armed defenders there and in some of the houses along the street immediately opened fire, and in the few moments of shooting four nativists lay dead and eleven others fell wounded. The remaining nativists with a stomach for a fight retreated to the Nanny Goat Market for shelter, and it seemed that the pattern of the day before would repeat itself. This time, however, the nativists changed their tactics. Rather than try to shoot it out with the well-concealed Irish, the nativists snuck out of the market building and set fire to each of the houses from which gunfire had been coming. This tactic proved successful as hidden Irish snipers came tumbling out of

4. Feldberg, p. 108.

the flaming buildings. They made easy targets for nativist gunners, and only poor nativist marksmanship explains why no Irishmen were killed. It was not until 5:00 P.M., nearly an hour after the shooting started, that General Cadwalader, previously unprepared, arrived with several militia companies to restore order in the neighborhood.

The use of fire struck panic in the hearts of the remaining Kensington Irish, and by Wednesday morning most of them had packed their possessions and gone elsewhere to stay with friends and relatives, or to camp in the woods on the outskirts of Philadelphia. The militia was left to guard their abandoned homes, but the outnumbered soldiers were inadequate for the task. Roving bands of nativists snuck from house to house in the vicinity of the Nanny Goat Market and set each on fire. The city's volunteer firefighters, mostly native-born Americans, had little enthusiasm for fighting the flames. In addition, after setting up a diversion to draw the militia away, a group of arsonists gained access to St. Michael's Roman Catholic Church, whose priest had been an outspoken foe of nativism, and set it to the torch. Flames rapidly devoured the wooden structure, and as the cross fell from the toppling steeple the crowd cheered loudly. Volunteer firefighters, arriving on the scene, determined that the gathering would never permit them to extinguish the fire, so they contented themselves with hosing down nearby buildings to keep the flames from spreading. Other rioters completed the day's work by ransacking two stores that had been selling ammunition to Irish marksmen, and eventually they invaded the home of Hugh Clark, the man whose decision to suspend Bible reading in Louisa Bedford's class had provided the pretext for the fighting. The invaders threw Clark's valuable books and furniture into the street and used them to start a bonfire. Finally, several hours after the arson had begun in Kensington, General Cadwalader and Sheriff McMichael arrived with reinforcements and brought the wandering rioters under control.

Thus blocked, the angry nativists simply transferred their field of activity to downtown Philadelphia. By 10:30 that Wednesday night, a huge crowd had gathered in front of St. Augustine's Roman Catholic Church in the heart of that city. Although the mayor stood on the building's front steps and pleaded with the crowd to disperse, his appeals went unheard. Someone knocked him down by heaving a stone against his chest, and a young boy managed to sneak past the constables at a rear door and set the church afire. Within half an hour the $45,000 brick structure was a total loss. As the steeple fell, the crowd cheered as it had done at St. Michael's. Again the volunteer firemen dared only hose down nearby buildings.

The burning of St. Augustine's marked the last major violence in the Kensington phase of the Native American Riots. Governor David R. Porter placed Philadelphia under martial law, and the chief commander of the Pennsylvania militia, General Robert Patterson, took complete command of the city's government. More than 2,000 soldiers from across the state patrolled the streets of Philadelphia, and General Patterson banned all meetings and demonstrations. Patterson instructed his men that they were "to use all force at their disposal to protect public and private property," that they were to "clear and occupy any street, alley, or private property to prevent riot, disturbance, or destruction." If the soldiers encountered resistance they were to issue a warning to the offenders, and then the streets were to be "cleared forcibly." The general closed his instructions with a clear threat to future rioters:

> Order must be restored, life and property rendered secure. The idle, the vicious, the disorderly must be curbed and taught to understand and respect the supremacy of the law and, if they do not take warning, on their own heads be the consequences.[5]

Martial law remained in effect for a week without a serious confrontation between troops and civilians, after which civilian government was restored to Philadelphia. Thus ended the Kensington phase of the 1844 Native American Riots.

5. Feldberg, p. 115.

# 2. The Philadelphia Riots of 1844:

# The Southwark Phase

The Kensington Riots had been the worst in Philadelphia's history. At least six persons had been killed, and as many as fifty had been seriously injured. Property losses in the three days of violence were conservatively estimated at $250,000, not counting the cost of medical bills and lost time from work.

While unusually destructive, the Kensington riots were in other ways typical of collective violence in the Jacksonian period. First, despite the fact that there was gunfire and killing in the first two days of fighting, it appears that only a relatively small portion of combatants on either side was armed. There is no way for us to know how many Philadelphians owned firearms in 1844, although rifles for hunting seem to have been quite common, and ammunition was widely sold in shops around the city. One of the stores set aflame by the crowd in Kensington, Corr's Grocery, was burned because its proprieter had been supplying bullets to his Irish compatriots. Jacksonian cities seem to have had no legal regulations about who could own, sell, or distribute guns or ammunition. Yet the use of guns by rioters was rarely reported in contemporary newspaper accounts. Crowds usually fought by hurling rocks, paving stones, bricks, and garbage, or by wielding clubs, knives, and slingshots. As a result, it was the exception rather than the rule for pre-Civil War rioting to claim the lives of its victims, or for more than one or two persons to be killed in the course of even the most serious fighting. During the three days and nights of the Kensington riots, for example, only one Irishman was killed, and he was an innocent bystander.

Second, the pattern of damage to property in Kensington indicates that, like most Jacksonian crowds, the nativist rioters exercised a good deal of restraint in their attacks. Despite their anger over the school Bible issue, the ambush at the Nanny Goat Market, and the murders of Schiffler and the others, it was not until Wednesday, two days after the outbreak of fighting, that widespread destruction was inflicted on Irish property. Before then only a few houses that had served as shelters for Irish snipers were targeted for burning. Other houses were stoned or damaged, but these too were suspected of harboring Irish marksmen. Even the choice of targets on Wednesday, when widespread arson was employed, was hardly random: Hugh Clark's house, his brother's tavern, Corr's Grocery, and two Catholic churches. Some additional homes may have been deliberately burned, especially in the area around the Nanny Goat Market, but many others fell unintended victim to the spreading flames. Rioters even bypassed the home of one elderly Irishman when they found him inside, too ill to make his escape. However much their anger had been provoked, the nativist rioters never rampaged through Kensington randomly destroying property or retaliating against whoever fell to hand. There was, in short, no orgy of irrational nativist fury. The rioters possessed clearly defined notions of what and who their targets ought to have been and why those targets deserved to suffer violence. While no one would argue that either the nativist or Irish rioters were acting dispassionately during the fighting, neither can one say that the rioters were insane, deranged, animalistic, or totally without sense or reason.

Third, the social composition of both sides in the Kensington riots was characteristic of that in many other Jacksonian riots. Contrary to many current stereotypes of rioters and looters, the Kensington combatants were not drawn from the poorest or most oppressed strata of Jacksonian society. The names of those injured or arrested, when traced to city directories, indicate that the rioters, frequently boys and young men in their twenties, were often employed as apprentice artisans, weavers, or laborers. They were not poverty-stricken outcasts, nor were they without a permanent residence. Many of the older men and women who participated on both sides were established members of their communities. Among the Irish there were property-owners, landlords, and employers who became as caught up in the heat of battle as their less affluent fellow immigrants. On the nativist side there were respectable American Republican lawyers, doctors, and dentists, as well as some constables and other elected officials. They fought alongside the youthful working-class members of nativist street gangs and volunteer fire companies notorious for their rowdy and combative behavior. What motivated rioters on both sides was not alienation, a sense of economic oppression, or a feeling of having "nothing to lose," but rather a deep commitment to their ethnic heritage and their political cause, intensified by their anger over the course of events that unfolded at the Nanny Goat Market. Tellingly, in three days of fighting and destruction, there was only one reported instance of looting. When rioters removed property from an Irish shop or Hugh Clark's home, it was to destroy it, not to keep it.

Fourth, the Kensington riots illustrate the intertwining of Jacksonian era collective violence with other, more peaceable forms of political and social behavior. The competition between immigrant Irish Catholics and native Protestant American Republicans began as a cultural controversy over the use of the Bible as a reading text in the public schools. It became a political issue when Hugh Clark convinced Louisa Bedford to remove the King James version from her class's daily lesson. After that, American Republicans began campaigning over the issue of "foreign interference" in the public schools, and when they carried this political campaign to Third Ward, Kensington, the debate changed from a clash of words to a clash of arms. As the next three chapters will demonstrate, the transition from cultural conflict to political conflict to physical conflict was all too frequent in Jacksonian group relations.

That the school Bible controversy shifted from a battle of petitions before the School Controllers to a battle of weapons in the streets of Kensington is stark testimony to the power of ethnic and religious issues to stir the passions of Philadelphians in 1844. It is also indicative, however, of the fifth and final factor common to most Jacksonian riots: the inability of public officials to prevent or suppress riots before they required the intervention of military troops. How strange it would seem today if, like Philadelphians on May 7, 1844, we awoke to find the walls, lampposts, and fences of our city or town plastered with calls for us to arm ourselves and attend a rally in order to seek revenge for the death of one of our fellow citizens. Then, once we arrived, we would find *no police officers* present to control the crowd or disarm its members. The current form of urban policing, in which uniformed officers actively patrol the streets searching out crime and disorder, and in which the police routinely patrol any political or protest rally prepared to disperse the crowd at the first sign of violence, was simply unknown in Jacksonian America.

"Preventive policing," as Jacksonians came to call it, was not introduced in Philadelphia until the 1850s. Like its sister cities Boston and New York, Philadelphia in 1844 still maintained public order through a system of constables, watchmen, and sheriff's posses whose origins dated back to the Middle Ages. The constables and watchmen, who neither pursued a preventive patrol strategy nor were given many incentives to control disorder, where ineffective against all but the smallest riots. Both the sheriff's posse and its backup, the state militia, possessed more manpower than the constabulary, but hours and sometimes days were needed to assemble their volunteer members, bring them to the scene of a disturbance, and turn them loose on the rioters. As civilians rather than professional law enforcement officers, the volunteers had little formal discipline, disliked taking orders, and sometimes openly sympathized with the rioters. Evidence suggests that the reluctance of some militia officers and troops to enter Kensington to save an Irish Catholic neighborhood might account for General Cadwalader's delay in responding to the rioting on the first two days. Because of rumor to this effect in the weeks after the Kensington fighting, Cadwalader and his men were quietly criticized by word-of-mouth among the city's leading elements. A proud, brave, and impetuous man who liked fast horses and beautiful women, Cadwalader was stung by these imputations on his personal courage and his control over his men. Consequently, he resolved that, at the next opportunity, he would show the citizens of Philadelphia what he and his men were made of. His opportunity would present itself in early July.

When the American Republican Party announced that it would hold a gala parade to celebrate the Fourth of July, Philadelphians anxiously awaited the day—either in anticipation of a great outpouring of patriotism or in fear of renewed fighting and violence between nativists and the immigrant Irish. Catholics, of course, feared that bitter nativists would use the holiday as a pretext for burning more churches. The American Republicans, however, were quite sensitive to their new reputation as "church burners," and they worked hard to see that the day was not marred by disorder. Sheriff McMichael, General Cadwalader, and other friends of public order prepared for potential violence by readying deputies, militiamen, and citizen volunteers to patrol the streets and nip any outbreak of violence before it blossomed into a riot. One such preventive step—a fateful one, it turned out—

was taken by the parishioners of St. Philip de Neri Roman Catholic Church in Southwark, a district just south of central Philadelphia. Its pastor, Father Peter Dunn, had heard a rumor that nativists were planning to attack the church on the Fourth, and so Father Dunn's brother William quietly approached Governor Porter for permission to form the Catholic men of Southwark into a volunteer militia company. The governor agreed, and as was common practice at the time, Dunn and his men were allowed to draw rifles from the state arsenal.

The Fourth itself passed peacefully, much to the relief of everyone involved. Almost 5,000 nativists paraded through the streets, and perhaps as many as 100,000 persons cheered from the sidewalks, windows, and rooftops of the city. Catholics either stayed home or maintained a low profile during the festivities. Unfortunately, though, the fifth was not to pass as quietly. That morning, the rifles ordered for the defense of St. Philip de Neri Church were seen arriving at the building's rear door, and word spread quickly through Southwark that the church was being armed in preparation for a Catholic attack on native Americans. A crowd quickly gathered and demanded that the arms be removed. Sheriff McMichael hurried to the scene with two local aldermen, entered the church, and learned that William Dunn was indeed authorized to arm a volunteer militia company. McMichael persuaded Dunn that his safest course was to calm the crowd by depositing the guns in the nearby Southwark Commissioners' Hall. Dunn agreed, and when the guns were carried off, most of those gathered dispersed. McMichael gathered some friends into a posse to guard the church, and General Cadwalader sent a company of soldiers to reinforce the men during the night.

Saturday morning, the soldiers and deputies faced an ever-enlarging crowd of curious and suspicious onlookers. At 2 P.M., General Cadwalader appeared in person at the church and ordered the throng to disperse. When those assembled hooted him down, Cadwalader lost his temper and huffed off, threatening to return with a major show of force. The crowd scoffed at him and continued to mill peacefully outside the church building. True to his word, Cadwalader indeed returned with several companies of soldiers and three light cannons. He ordered his men to fix bayonets and clear the streets. While the troops herded the crowd, some of the bolder protestors started throwing rocks at them and loudly proclaimed their right to gather in the public streets. Cadwalader issued a final warning for the crowd to disperse at once or face the blasts of his soldiers' cannons and rifles. He then gave the order to "ready, aim, fire!" At that very moment, Southwark politician Charles Naylor stepped forward, stood before the pointed rifles and yelled, "My God, don't shoot! Don't shoot!"[1]

Distracted by Naylor's plea, Cadwalader's men refrained from firing, and the crowd had a chance to melt away. But the general was furious. He immediately ordered Naylor and twenty straggling protestors placed under arrest and held in the church basement. Thus Saturday night, July 5, ended without bloodshed, but only by the narrowest of margins. Sunday was to prove less fortunate.

Trouble was renewed on Sunday morning when a group of nativists, led by two Southwark aldermen, appeared at St. Philip's to demand the release of Naylor and his fellow prisoners. Two companies of militia— one composed of Irish immigrants and the other of native Americans— had been left to guard the prisoners, but the soldiers were badly outnumbered by the crowd. After sending Cadwalader a plea for reinforcements—which did not arrive for several hours—Captain John Colahan, the commander of the Irish company (who was in charge of the entire operation), agreed to let the prisoners, including Naylor, be released into the custody of the aldermen. Colahan did not trust the willingness of the soldiers in the native American company to protect the church, and he feared that if he did not meet the protestors' demands and if reinforcements did not arrive, his men would be overwhelmed and perhaps killed. Colahan was then persuaded to remove his men

1. Quoted in Michael Feldberg, *The Philadelphia Riots of 1844: A Study of Ethnic Conflict* (Westport, Conn., 1975), p. 148.

from the church and to turn it over for safekeeping to volunteer American Republican activists, who swore to guard the building against all harm. As the Irish soldiers withdrew, portions of the crowd pelted them with rocks, and in response one of the soldiers opened fire. He was beaten by the crowd and mistakenly left for dead. The other soldiers ran, escaping without serious injury. The area around the church remained crowded with curious onlookers, mostly nativists, but the church itself was securely guarded by a group of American Republican volunteers. Again, the party was trying to live down its "church burners" reputation, and so the most widely known American Republicans made it their business to stand watch over St. Philip's while the crowd surged outside the building.

As darkness fell on this turbulent but nonviolent scene, General Cadwalader arrived with the heavily armed reinforcements that Captain Colahan had requested. To his surprise, Cadwalader found not Colahan's soldiers but a group of American Republicans in charge of the church, and that his prisoners, especially Charles Naylor, were gone. Outraged, he commanded the American Republicans out of the building and called on his troops to clear the streets. With swords drawn and bayonets fixed, the soldiers began to push the crowds away from the church. The civilians answered with rocks, brickbats, and occasional gunshots. Cadwalader ordered his men to return the fire. This time no one stepped forward to save the crowd. The soldiers' first volley killed two men and wounded four others. The crowd fled in terror. Some went to their homes, many to return with guns in order to seek revenge on Cadwalader and his men. Under the cover of night a group of young men went to a nearby dock and removed two cannons from a Navy ship anchored at the federal dockyard, fully prepared to do battle with the soldiers.

The nativists' cannons proved effective for a while. The first blast killed two soldiers and injured several more. The next time the insurgents fired at the troops, though, Cadwalader called for cavalry reinforcements, and a detachment of horsemen quickly galloped up, killed two of the gunners, and captured the weapon. After that the nativists were afraid to fire the other cannon for fear of revealing its position, and while the soldiers supposedly rode past it several times during the night, the weapon lay idle. Instead, the nativists kept up a sporadic rifle fire until dawn, but the major fighting had ceased. The military had suffered two dead and twenty-three wounded, the rioters approximately ten dead and twenty or more injured.

Once again Governor Porter imposed martial law on Philadelphia and soldiers occupied the streets of Southwark. Nativist hatred of the soldiers was unbounded; as soldiers fainted from thirst in the intense July heat, no Southwark residents offered them water. As General Cadwalader later recalled, "the houses of the people were closed against us."[2] The nativist dead of Southwark were buried with great fanfare and honor by local residents, and relations between the military and civilians were at the flash point. Acting on the advice of the Southwark commissioners, General Patterson, under whose command the district was placed, agreed to withdraw the troops and restore civilian government. The troops left, no further violence occurred, and St. Philip's church was no longer threatened.

Respectable Philadelphians of all religions and political beliefs were left in a state of shock by their realization that civil war between the military and citizens had broken out on the city's streets. The deaths of soldiers and civilians seemed to sober Irish and nativists alike. There was no more rioting in Philadelphia over the issue of the Bible in the public schools after July 7, 1844, although street fighting between native and Irish gangs and fire companies did continue until the eve of the Civil War. Thus ended the great Philadelphia Native American Riots of 1844.

2. Feldberg, p. 157.

# 3. Varieties of Jacksonian Violence:

# Preservatist Riots

The Southwark riots proved to be the exception rather than the rule in pre-Civil War collective violence. As had been the case in Kensington, Jacksonian riots usually pitted two rival groups in direct confrontation with each other. The anti-black, anti-immigrant, and anti-Mormon rioting that will be discussed in this chapter each followed the Kensington pattern. In other riots, an isolated individual or a small group of individuals was attacked by the rioters. Riots involving anti-abolitionists and vigilante mobs are examples of this type of conflict. The Jacksonian period, however, also produced a smaller group of riots that, like the Southwark confrontation, matched an angry or excited private group against a sheriff's posse or a company of militia troops. Labor and economic riots, discussed in Chapter Four, clearly demonstrate this type of encounter.

There are criteria other than the nature of opponents or victims by which we can classify Jacksonian collective violence. We may divide Jacksonian riots into those that were intended to further a group's political cause, and those that were intended primarily to fulfill a group's emotional or recreational needs. We may choose to separate these riots into those that advanced the cause of social or political change, and those that were intended to preserve the status quo. For the most part, the riots discussed in this chapter were *preservatist,* that is, they were attempts by groups that held some degree of economic, social, or political power to maintain their privileged position over groups below them on the social ladder. Preservatist riots, then, were highly political in nature, if the term "political" is understood not merely as an electoral process, but as a social process by which groups compete for the material and prestige rewards that their society has to offer. By contrast, Chapter Four will explore those riots that had a predominantly expressive or recreational rather than preservatist, political character.

The major categories of rioting discussed in this chapter are religious and ethnic rioting, rioting that concerns racial violence, and rioting that involves anti-abolition mobs. Each category will be explored in a separate section, and the ways in which the rioters used violence will be indicated. Not surprisingly, there were some overlaps in form, purpose, or results among the categories. Throughout this and the following chapter, the reader should remember that the formal distinctions made here are often drawn more sharply than is warranted by the complex historical reality that they are meant to represent.

## Religious and Ethnic Rioting

The Philadelphia riots of 1844 were hardly an isolated instance of ethnic or religious conflict. The 1830s and 1840s were punctuated by at least a dozen other major riots between ethnic or religious rivals, as well as by numerous less dramatic incidents. In 1834 religious hostility toward Catholics appeared in Charlestown, Massachusetts, just outside Boston, when a crowd led by "neighborhood truckmen" invaded and burned a convent school near the site of Bunker Hill. Boston itself was the scene of the 1837 Broad Street Riot, which broke out when native Protestant volunteer firefighters, returning from a run, crossed paths with an Irish Catholic funeral procession. Neither side would yield the right of way, and this led to an exchange of words and then blows between the two groups. When troops finally separated them, several persons were lying in the street badly injured. In 1838 several Mormons were murdered by angry Missourians who resented the Mormon leaders' advocacy of plural marriage and the immunity of their followers from the laws of the United States. In 1844 Mormon Prophet Joseph Smith and his brother Hyrum were massacred by a lynch mob as they sat imprisoned in a Nauvoo, Illinois, jail. After this atrocity, Mormons and "Gentiles" (as the Mormons called their non-Mormon neighbors) fought a continuing guerrilla war until the Mormons relocated in the sparsely populated wilds of Utah. In 1858 anywhere from fourteen to one hundred German immigrants were killed in Louisville, Kentucky, during an outbreak of anti-German rioting. Even in places as remote as Ellsworth, Maine, in 1854 a Catholic priest was tarred and feathered by a mob.

As the chapter on the 1844 Philadelphia riots had already hinted, it is difficult to say whether the warfare between immigrants and nativists in the 1830s, 1840s, and 1850s was primarily religious or ethnic. That is, were the Irish made targets of nativist violence because they were immigrants who had alien social customs, drinking habits, and crime patterns, or because they were Catholics who believed in a competing version of Christianity? Were they victimized as newcomers to the United States because they possessed separatist attitudes and unfamiliar speech patterns, or were they simply scapegoats for ancient Protestant hatreds that were born in the era of the European Reformation?

Some evidence points to the fact that Catholicism was a less important factor than Irishness, for—the Louisville episode aside—German

Catholics seem to have suffered less violence and discrimination than the Irish. During the Philadelphia riots, for example, nativists marched right past a German Catholic church on their way to burn St. Augustine's, which had an Irish congregation. The parish church in Irish immigrant neighborhoods served not only as a house of worship but also as a community center, so that nativist resentment of Irish immigrant separatism was often focused on parish churches in the same way that it was aimed at Irish taverns, fire houses, and other community meeting places such as Kensington's Nanny Goat Market.

It is also true, however, that Catholicism *as a religion* fired the wrath of many American Protestants, especially those belonging to the fundamentalist and evangelical wings of the Methodist, Baptist, and Presbyterian churches. A remote hamlet such as Ellsworth, Maine, surely did not suffer from an overwhelming Irish immigrant slum or crime problem. The unfortunate priest who received a coat of tar and feathers in 1854 was probably assaulted for his religious beliefs rather than for his national origins. Catholic doctrines, especially the notions of papal infallibility and priestly celibacy, came under constant attack from evangelical Protestant clergymen, who convinced many of their listeners that Catholicism was, at bottom, a hostile conspiracy threatening Protestantism and the American way of life.

It has been suggested that nativists, evangelicals, anti-Mormons, and others who feared "alien" religious or political conspiracies against American institutions were actually searching for a "sense of self-identity and personal direction in an otherwise rootless and shifting environment." Participation in anti-immigrant, anti-Mormon, anti-Catholic, or other patriotic crusades offered Jacksonians a "sense of common dedication to a noble and sacred tradition."[1] These preserva-

---

1. David Brion Davis, "Some Themes of Countersubversion: An Analysis of Anti-Masonic, Anti-Catholic, and Anti-Mormon Literature," *The Mississippi Valley Historical Review* 47 (September 1960): 205–224. Quoted in Richard O. Curry and Thomas M. Brown, eds., *Conspiracy: The Fear of Subversion in American History* (New York, 1972), pp. 65, 69.

tist movements thus provided Protestant Americans with an antidote to their disorientation and anxiety as they tried to cope with the disruptive trends of their day: rapid population increases, technological and economic changes, and challenges to native Protestant cultural and moral dominance. This view assumes that the active violence and rioting against immigrants, Mormons, and Catholics offered nativists and fundamentalists a physical outlet for their psychological tensions.

But collective violence can serve other functions besides psychological ones. By murdering Joseph Smith and making war on his followers, Nauvoo's anti-Mormons achieved some tangible results. They were able to rid Illinois of the unwelcome Mormon settlement, since within months of the violence Brigham Young led the Mormons to the wastelands of Utah. Nativist attacks on Philadelphia's Irish Catholics probably encouraged later Irish immigrants to gravitate toward Boston and New York. Put another way, such things as housing, job opportunities, control of political power, and other social benefits have been the constant object of competition among America's ethnic, religious, racial, and cultural groups. Jacksonian collective violence should be understood as one of the means by which some established groups attempted to preserve or expand their power, their privilege, their sense of moral superiority, and their access to material advantages.

## Racial Rioting

Mormons and Catholics were not the only ones who felt the sting of preservatist group attacks on their communities. Perhaps no group withstood more collective violence in northern cities than free blacks. Racism has been a part of American culture since the founding of the colonies. Various explanations have been offered to account for American racism: psychological and sexual fears; the need to find scapegoats; or class competition. Ultimately, the sources of American racism, like other forms of prejudice, remain difficult to isolate. Its manifestations, however, are never far from sight. During the Jacksonian era, discrimination against blacks flourished in the cities of the North as well as on the plantations of the South. Counterposed to the whippings and punishments of southern slaves were the race riots aimed against northern free blacks.

Racial violence was quite common in Jacksonian cities: between 1832 and 1849, Philadelphia alone experienced five major and numerous smaller interracial battles. Other cities had only slightly better records. An 1829 attack on "Bucktown," the black portion of Cincinnati, drove half the black population—some 1,200 to 1,400 persons—from that city. In 1804 and 1807, the Ohio legislature passed Black Laws compelling Negroes who entered the state to prove that they were freedmen and forcing them to post a $500 bond to guarantee their good behavior. The law was left virtually unenforced until the late 1820s, when white public opinion in Cincinnati became aroused by a rapid influx of blacks into the city. The municipal government, feeling pressured by local voters, announced its intention to apply the laws, and told blacks that they had thirty days either to comply or leave. A delegation of black leaders obtained an extension of the enforcement period while they sought a suitable place of refuge in Canada.

Cincinnati's anti-black citizens, however, had little patience for such a delay. Anxious to purge blacks from the city, mobs of whites numbering in the hundreds rampaged through "Bucktown," destroying furniture, burning houses, stealing property, and scattering the inhabitants. The rioting lasted for three days, killing one black and injuring many others. The riots petered out of their own accord, but the hostile atmosphere convinced large numbers of Cincinnati's blacks to settle in Canada.

Our contemporary image of race riots derives from the ghetto uprisings of the 1960s. Television screens across the nation portrayed blacks in Watts, Harlem, Detroit, and Newark rampaging through their own neighborhoods, destroying homes and shops, and fighting gun battles with police and soldiers, all in rebellion against social, legal, and economic injustices. But this form of racial rioting dates only from the 1940s. In Jacksonian America, racial outbreaks followed the Cincinnati pattern: whites invaded a black neighborhood, beat unfortunate black victims, tore down or burned houses and public buildings, and sometimes killed those blacks who chose to resist the invasion and destruction of their communities. Inevitably, when blacks fought back, whites responded by redoubling their fury, bringing even greater disaster down on the black minority.

The burden blacks faced in defending themselves from white rioters is illustrated by an 1842 racial disturbance that occurred in the Philadelphia suburb of Moyamensing. On August 1 of that year, a Negro temperance society organized a parade to celebrate Jamaican Emancipation Day. During the parade, marchers carried a banner depicting a black slave breaking his chains against a background of a rising sun, which was meant to symbolize the dawning of freedom. Some of Moyamensing's Irish immigrants took offense at the banner; they later claimed that they thought the image of the sun advocated the fiery death of the white race. Whether or not they actually believed this, the Irish spectators obviously welcomed a battle, as they pelted the black marchers with fruits and vegetables.

Serious fighting began as the blacks were driven out of the Irish district and into their own ghetto. The sheriff arrived with a posse and arrested twenty combatants, most of them black. The few whites arrested were rescued from the hands of the unarmed sheriff's deputies by the crowds. Fighting subsided by late morning, but in early afternoon a gunshot from the home of a black resident wounded a white teenager, and soon a crowd of more than a thousand persons was pillaging the neighborhood around St. Mary's Street. Several blacks were severely beaten, and the crowd burned the black temperance meeting hall and the Presbyterian church. Hundreds of blacks fled Moyamensing, seeking shelter in Philadelphia's police stations or anywhere that they could find it. The following morning, when some black stevedores reported for work at the Schuylkill river wharves, immigrant Irish dockworkers trapped them in a warehouse and threatened to burn it down. Sheriff William Porter sent sixty of his deputies to rescue the blacks. Hundreds of whites joined the dockworkers in driving the posse away with rocks, clubs, and pistols, and eventually seven militia companies had to be summoned to Moyamensing to restore order.

An interesting sidelight to the 1842 anti-temperance riot arose the following winter. A few years earlier, the Philadelphia county commissioners had adopted an ordinance stating that individuals or corporations who lost property during a riot could apply for reimbursement from each district's treasury. Under this ordinance, the black owners of the burned temperance meeting hall applied to the commissioners of Moyamensing for compensation. The commissioners denied their request. When asked to explain why they would not pay the black temperance organization, the commissioners claimed that the marchers had brought the destruction on themselves; they should have known, the commissioners argued, that a march to celebrate Jamaican Emancipation would tend to excite the passions of the white population of Moyamensing. Such was the consequence paid by those blacks who chose to exercise their rights of free assembly and free speech.

Moyamensing in particular seemed to suffer from a volatile mix of black and white residents, many if not most of whom were poor. The area was known for its Irish immigrants, recently arrived blacks, sleazy taverns, gambling dens, prostitutes, interracial marriages, street gangs, criminals, and, above all, poverty. Matthew Carey, a humanitarian observer, reported in 1838 that on a stroll through Moyamensing, "the heart sickens, and the feelings revolt at the scenes of degradation and misery which constantly meet our view." During the 1832 cholera epidemic, observers reported discovering literally hundreds of "men, women and children, black and white, barefooted, lame and blind, half-naked and dirty." Ironically, the material equality of the races in Moyamensing did not exempt the district's whites from the universal white prejudice that the Negro's "place in society should be inferior to that of the least favored white man." As the "least favored" of the nation's whites, the immigrant Irish were especially susceptible to such reasoning. As an English traveler observed of the American Irish in 1833, "nearly all of them, who have resided here at any length of time, are more bitter and severe against the blacks than the native whites themselves. It seems as if the disease were more virulent when taken by inoculation than in the natural way."[2]

The Moyamensing "Flying Horses" riot of 1834 illustrates the impact of the district's social disorganization, poverty, criminality, and racial competition. The fighting began on the night of August 12, which had been by most accounts "the hottest and most oppressive day we have had this summer." The outbreak at the "Flying Horses," a carousel on the border of Moyamensing that was attracting both black and white customers, had been preceeded on August 8 by a fight between a group of blacks and the members of the Fairmount Engine Company, a group known for its tendency to riot. The next evening, "a gang of fifty or sixty young men in blue jackets and trousers, and low crowned straw hats" attacked the son of Philadelphia's most eminent black. The gang vowed to meet again on the eleventh, when they planned to "attack the niggers." While nothing happened that night, on the twelfth a mob of several hundred whites attacked the Flying Horses, beat and scattered the black patrons, and wrecked the building and the carousel. The crowd then roamed through Moyamensing, imposing havoc and destruction on the neighborhood. For three nights the rioting remained uncontrolled by public officials. The damage to black property on the second night of rioting, according to the Philadelphia *Inquirer,* "exceeds belief—No less than thirty-seven houses,

2. The quotations in this and the following paragraph were taken from John Runcie, "'Hunting the Nigs' in Philadelphia: The Race Riot of August 1834," *Pennsylvania History* 39 (April 1972): 191–192, 198, 212–213, 215, 216.

some of them substantial brick tenements, were more or less destroyed, and many of them rendered entirely uninhabitable." Crowds
looted the property of blacks, pocketing silverware and cash, burning
or breaking what they could not carry. "The furniture of the houses
was broken into the smallest fragments; nothing escaped; the bedding
was carried into the street, ripped up with knives, and the contents
scattered far and wide. The bedsteads, chairs and tables were hacked to
chips." People as well as property suffered at the mob's hands. One
black was killed, many were badly hurt, and the constabulary suffered
several injuries as well. A reporter for the Philadelphia *Gazette* noted
that, "The mob exhibited more than fiendish brutality, beating and
mutilating some of the old, confiding and unoffending blacks, with a
savageness surpassing anything we could have believed men capable
of."

The irrational hate and fury heaped on the blacks of Moyamensing
was reflective of the general northern attitude toward blacks in Jacksonian America. It is impossible to count just how many attacks there
were on northern blacks in the 1830s and 1840s. Incidents on the scale
of the Bucktown invasion or the Flying Horses riots seem to have
happened dozens of times in northern cities; other less extensive
events, such as the attack on the black temperance marchers, or even
smaller scuffles, gang fights, and individual beatings, were yet more
common. Obviously, free northern blacks shared many of the insecuri-
ties, pains, and injuries borne by their southern slave brethren.

Still, there was a difference between the collective violence aimed at
slaves in the South and that suffered by free blacks in the North. The
response to Nat Turner's rebellion, near Hampton, Virginia, was the
one major instance of southern *collective* racial violence (as opposed to
the whipping and beating of individual slaves) in the Jacksonian era.
Nat Turner was a charismatic slave preacher who led his fellow slaves
in a short-lived uprising in which the rebel slaves took the lives of
Turner's master and several other whites. In retaliation, the white
people of the Hampton area declared open warfare on Turner, his
followers, and any other slaves who might have been contaminated by

his teachings. Vigilante lynch mobs, clothed with the authority of law, hunted down runaway and fearful blacks, both slave and free. When the killing was ended and Turner finally captured, whites had hanged or shot at least fifty blacks. The furious response to Turner's uprising made a deep impression on other slaves: His was the last organized large-scale rebellion by southern slaves prior to the outbreak of the Civil War.

Racial violence in the Jacksonian years served, both North and South, as a means by which whites intimidated blacks and enjoyed a sense of domination over them. With the exception of Nat Turner's rebellion, pre-Civil War race rioting was not, as it has been in our day, a manifestation of black discontent with a racist society. Rather, the aggressors in racial collective violence were whites. In the North white rioting was a clear reminder to blacks to "stay in their place." Northern whites might not have owned slaves, but they could use rioting to prove to themselves that northern blacks were as powerless as their slave brothers.

## Anti-Abolitionist Violence

During the 1830s, riots against abolitionists were numerically the most common form of collective violence. As noted in the introduction, there were literally hundreds of attacks on abolitionists in 1834, 1835, and 1836 alone, and many others doubtlessly went unreported. Because they advocated an immediate end to slavery with no compensation to former masters and without sending the freed slaves off to Africa, the abolitionists were viewed by the vast majority of Jacksonian Americans as radicals. Not only their views but their tactics seemed revolutionary. Abolitionists were masters at using the newly invented mass printing techniques of the age: the handbill, the short pamphlet, the penny press, the printed illustration of a slave bound in chains or of a master beating a female field hand. They used financial donations by their most affluent northern supporters to print millions of handbills

and flood the mails and churches with them. Much of their propaganda
was aimed at the consciences of women and children, and the abolitionists scandalized most of their white male contemporaries by invit-
ing women to join in local anti-slavery societies. Most anti-abolitionists
and colonizationists (those persons who wished to ship freed slaves
back to Africa—and who wished to free them only as quickly as they
could be shipped back) were locally organized, and could not compete
with the nationwide abolitionist network. Therefore, collective violence
against abolitionists, the destruction of their printing presses, and the
burning or disrupting of their mailings became a convenient and
effective technique for combatting the abolition crusade.

On the surface, anti-abolitionist rioting was blatantly racist: Attacks
on white anti-slavery advocates were intended to show American blacks
that, despite the support of a few misguided friendly whites, a slave or
an ex-slave could never become the social, political, or economic equal of
a free white American. Northern anti-abolition mobs made it very clear
that freed blacks were unwelcome in their cities and towns. But the
abolitionists' methods and philosophies provoked politically preservatist as well as racist reactions from their fellow northern whites. Unlike
most other forms of Jacksonian collective violence, anti-abolition riots
often involved sizable proportions of community leaders and respectable middle- and upper-class citizens. This "better" class of Jacksonians—one historian has called them "gentlemen of property and
standing"—continued to support colonization as a solution to the
slavery issue. Colonizationists in most cities tended to belong to
traditional political elites, and this older class of influentials resented
the inroads made by the abolitionists' modern propaganda techniques.
To a large degree, anti-abolition leaders were battling to retain their
traditional control over local political opinion, church organizations,
schools, and the racial beliefs of women and children. In sum, there
was more at stake in northern anti-abolitionist violence than the
freedom of southern slaves.

While the abolition movement had been easily crushed in the South
by the early 1830s, it was expanding rapidly in the cities and towns of

the North. But northern anti-slavery agitators met opposition on several grounds. First, the abolitionists were loudly denouncing the morality of the American Constitution, since the document contained several clauses that, at least implicitly, recognized the legality of slavery. The best-known abolitionist leader, Boston's William Lloyd Garrison, went so far as to brand the Constitution a pact with the Devil. Anti-abolitionists were angered by such attacks, as well as by the abolitionists' denunciation of slavery as a form of property holding. If the Constitution could be changed to abolish slavery, anti-abolitionists argued, then no form of private property was safe.

Second, abolitionists appeared to threaten the security of the Union. With a logic later borne out by the Civil War, anti-abolitionists argued that anti-slavery agitation would provoke a break between the North and the South. By advocating their views in public, abolitionists could cause slave rebellions; southern whites would then feel that their best security lay in separation from a national government that permitted such threats to their social and economic way of life.

Third, anti-abolitionists were disturbed by the racial implications of the abolitionist call for immediate emancipation. Few white northerners would have welcomed an influx of freed blacks who, it was imagined, would come flooding northward in search of jobs and shelter. Anti-abolitionists feared, on a sexual level, that the army of migrant blacks would physically mix with the white population of the North, leading to "amalgamation," or what is known today as miscegenation. It was because they could not condone any physical mingling of the races that many northern whites supported colonization. Abolitionists rejected this plan outright on the grounds that American blacks had worked without pay to build America for more than two hundred years, and thus deserved a compensating share of the land and its wealth when they were freed.

Anti-abolition mobs fell into two broad categories: those that were planned and even announced in advance, and those that appear to have formed more spontaneously. Planned anti-abolition mobs were notable for their upper-class leadership and their moderate, even polite quality. Unlike the racial fury of the Flying Horses or the Bucktown riots, in which random destruction and injury were inflicted on large numbers of victims, the genteel form of anti-abolition rioting was intended to intimidate individual abolitionists and editors, not kill them or harm them permanently. A typical example of such organized anti-abolition rioting occurred in 1835 in Utica, New York. There, a crowd of "gentlemen of property and standing"—lawyers, doctors, bankers, merchants, tradesmen, and state and local politicians—disrupted a state abolitionist convention organized by Utica's anti-slavery society.

More than seven hundred anti-slavery advocates were expected at the Utica convention. Anti-abolitionists in that city and elsewhere were urged by local and state newspapers to "put down" the convention, either by the laws of New York or by the "law of Judge Lynch." The Utica grand jury had ruled a few days before that persons organizing anti-slavery societies were guilty of sedition, and that it was "the duty of all our citizens" who were "friendly to the Constitution" and the "future quiet and happiness of this people" to destroy anti-slavery literature *"whenever and wherever* found."[3] In short, the atmosphere surrounding the convention was already filled with threats against the abolitionists' right to free speech and free assembly.

Utica's anti-abolitionists were not reluctant to use violence in pursuit of their goals. At a rally on October 16, 1835, local newspaper editor Augustine G. Dauby told an excited crowd that he would "be here on that morning and do my duty manfully to prevent the meeting, *peacefully if I can, forcibly if I must."* When the convention was finally assembled in the Bleeker Street Church on the twenty-first, a "committee" of twenty-five respectable anti-abolitionists burst into the church, tore the coat off the back of one abolitionist, threw

3. Quotations from participants in the Utica riots taken from Leonard L. Richards, *"Gentlemen of Property and Standing": Anti-Abolition Mobs in Jacksonian America* (New York, 1970), pp. 86, 87, 90, 92.

hymnals, and tore up anti-slavery literature. They shouted down the meeting and forced the abolitionists to retreat to a fellow member's estate twenty-seven miles from Utica. That night, a crowd of angry demonstrators destroyed the offices of a Democratic newspaper that had supported the convention's right to meet. State Senator Silas Wright of New York City said later that the crowd's actions had shown "evidences of the correct state of public opinion," and two of the anti-abolitionist rioters were actually elected to state office in the ensuing months.

Another variant of planned anti-abolitionist rioting was inflicted on a young Quaker schoolmistress, Prudence Crandall, who in 1833 and 1834 attempted to establish a boarding school exclusively for black girls in Canterbury, Connecticut. Led by United States district judge Andrew T. Judson, the good people of Canterbury convinced the state legislature to outlaw such a school, and when Crandall defied the law by teaching her black students, she was convicted and sentenced to prison for her offense. An appeals court overturned her conviction in late 1834, and she resumed her educational efforts. Crandall's persistence literally drove the citizens of Canterbury to violence. Enemies stoned the school, on several occasions filled its well with manure, and eventually tried to burn it down. When, finally, on a September night in 1834, a crowd invaded her house and destroyed its contents, Crandall gave up the struggle and moved to Illinois.

Rarely in the hundreds of planned anti-abolitionist riots was a well-known abolitionist seriously hurt, and only one, newspaper editor Elijah P. Lovejoy, was killed. The circumstances of Lovejoy's death, however exceptional, are worth examining for what they tell us about the possibilities of serious injury and death in a Jacksonian riot.

In 1836, Lovejoy was invited by some of the citizens of Alton, Illinois, to transfer his newspaper to Alton from St. Louis, where he was involved in a public dispute over the subject of anti-slavery and the treatment of northern blacks. Lovejoy published in Alton for a year before openly endorsing abolitionism and calling for the formation of an Alton anti-slavery society. While Lovejoy had some support in the town, the majority of civic leaders seemed opposed to his campaign. They convened a meeting to oppose Lovejoy's editorial policies, hoping to discourage him from making further efforts at organizing Alton's abolitionists. When he would not desist, a secret committee of twelve, including three physicians, resolved to destroy Lovejoy's press, tar and feather him, place him on a boat, and sail him down the Mississippi. These men wavered in their decison to assault Lovejoy, but on August 21, 1837, they did destroy his printing press.

Lovejoy's supporters responded by ordering a new press. On September 21, the night of the press's arrival, a band of men took the press from its warehouse, removed it to the street, and began dismantling it. When Mayor John Krum arrived and asked the men to disperse, they replied that they would, as soon as the press was destroyed. Mayor Krum granted them time to finish. He later described them as an unusually "quiet and gentlemanly mob."[4]

After the destruction of the second press, Altonians debated whether Lovejoy and the abolitionists had a right to free speech, or whether popular opinion should dictate what was published in the town. The vast majority supported the argument of anti-abolition leaders that "the interests and feelings of the citizens of Alton should be consulted," and that abstract ideas such as free speech and freedom of the press were subordinate to the popular will. The abolitionists and their friends, in turn, obtained permission from Mayor Krum to arm themselves to protect Lovejoy and his third press, which had been ordered and was expected to arrive shortly. It came on November 7, in the middle of the night, and was unloaded into a stone warehouse that resembled a fortress. Lovejoy's opponents heard of its delivery, and immediately planned to storm the building and disassemble the press. Volunteer abolitionists and others who believed in free speech (or simply "law and order") assembled to defend the warehouse, but a large crowd of anti-abolitionists marched to the warehouse and demanded the press. As the leader of the crowd told the building's defenders, "We bear no ill feelings toward any of you, but we intend to get the press at the sacrifice of *our* lives!" Shortly thereafter, someone fired the first shot, and one of the anti-abolitionists fell dead in the ensuing shower of bullets.

The death of one of their number infuriated the crowd, which by now had determined not only to destroy the press but to avenge the loss of their compatriot. When the mayor asked Lovejoy and his defenders to save further bloodshed by surrendering the press, the abolitionists refused. Mayor Krum relayed their answer to the crowd, whose response was to make preparations to burn the warehouse with its occupants inside. Ladders were placed against the building and one of the attackers climbed to the roof with a flaming torch. Lovejoy and a companion raced from the building in an attempt to shoot the arsonist, and in the rain of gunfire returned by the crowd, Lovejoy was struck five times. He crawled back into the building and died at his supporters' feet. With Lovejoy dead the defenders dispersed. A handful of anti-abolitionists entered the building, dropped the press from a third floor window, carried it to the river, dismantled it, and hurled the pieces into the water. Others stayed behind to put out the fire and set the warehouse back in order. The leader of the crowd told his followers that he "did not want any property injured, nor anything taken away."

The distinction between the Utica or Canterbury crowds, which harmed no one, and the Alton crowd, which shot Lovejoy, stems not so much from the relative bloodthirstiness of the Alton rioters, but from the level of resistance mounted by their opponents. Utica, Canterbury, and Alton all produced well-organized, well-planned, and well-controlled crowds with responsible community leaders at their head. That the Alton episode produced bloodshed and death indicates that the number of casualties in a Jacksonian riot was not so much a function of the anger or excitement felt by a crowd, or the particular grievances that brought a crowd together, but rather was a function of the resistance that crowds encountered while pursuing their aims. This

4. Quotations from the Alton riots taken from Richards, pp. 105, 109, 110.

hypothesis is supported by the experiences of the black residents of St. Mary's Street in Moyamensing who chose to fight back when whites invaded their neighborhood, or of the Kensington Irish who fought the nativist invasion of the Nanny Goat Market in May, 1844, or of the Southwark nativists who battled the Pennsylvania militia that July. In riots where there was little or no resistance to the rioters, there were usually no fatalities and few injuries. When public officials tried to suppress angry rioters, or when the rioters' victims chose to defend themselves, the toll of dead and injured rose dramatically. As a general rule in Jacksonian riots, unopposed crowds usually gained their goals by harassing or injuring their victims or destroying some of their property. The mob then usually dispersed in a boisterous and happy mood. When rioters met resistance and a return of force, however, they were far more likely to grow angered, employ deadly weapons, and seek the blood of their victims. The stiffer the resistance, the more likely there was to be death or serious injury on both sides.

A substantial minority of anti-abolitionist crowds seem to have developed spontaneously, with little if any sign of planning or leadership on the part of "gentlemen of property and standing." Such crowds were more likely to appear in large cities such as New York, Boston, and Philadelphia. These rioters tended, among other things, to be composed of and led by individuals from working-class and immigrant backgrounds, to carry their attacks beyond abolitionists and onto blacks and black neighborhoods as their rioting progressed, and to indulge in more generalized destruction of property than did the better planned and organized mobs led by elite anti-abolitionists. In July 1834, for example, an anti-abolitionist crowd in New York City rioted for three days, destroying at least sixty dwellings and six churches. In 1841, a Cincinnati anti-abolition crowd turned its attention from an anti-slavery meeting to an entire black neighborhood, producing one death and at least thirty serious injuries. Perhaps the most dramatic big-city, anti-abolition riot occurred in Philadelphia: the 1838 burning of abolitionist-built Pennsylvania Hall. Of the thirteen persons arrested in that riot, all had Irish-sounding names and working-class occupations. While this may tell us more about the selectivity of the sheriff's posse that arrested the rioters than it proves about the absence of "gentlemen of property and standing," it seems clear from contemporary accounts that the burning of Pennsylvania Hall and the events that followed it happened without the planning and foreknowledge of Philadelphia's upper-class elite.

The story of Pennsylvania Hall begins in 1837, when the Pennsylvania Anti-Slavery Society decided to construct a headquarters for the national abolition movement. Philadelphia's abolitionists had been having difficulty finding accommodations large enough to house their printing presses and hold their meetings, so they raised money to erect a large hall near the center of the city. Abolitionists across the nation were proud of the Philadelphians' effort, and in May 1838 the new building was given a gala opening. The Pennsylvania Anti-Slavery Society sponsored a national anti-slavery convention and abolitionist luminaries William Lloyd Garrison and the Grimké sisters gave the keynote addresses. The four-day agenda included lectures on another radical cause, women's rights. But the organizers' worst offense in the eyes of many of their enemies was the fact that blacks and whites attended the lectures without segregation by race or sex, leaving the abolitionists open to the charge of encouraging "amalgamation."

For two days, meetings and lectures were carried on without disturbance, although the spectacle of blacks and whites entering and leaving the hall together certainly caused comment among anti-abolition and racist Philadelphians. Then, on the evening of May 16, when Angelina Grimké was addressing the Female Anti-Slavery Society, a small group of agitators threw rocks at the building's windows. The mayor had assigned two constables to protect the hall, and its managers asked him for additional protection at the following day's events. When the mayor claimed that he lacked the legal powers or resources to guard the building adequately, the owners decided to cancel the remainder of the program. A crowd of 3,000 gathered that night nonetheless, and despite pleas for order by the mayor and the sheriff, hundreds surged forward, battered down the doors, and set the hall on fire. Firefighters rushed to the scene but chose only to keep the flames from spreading to nearby buildings.

The next night, while neither the sheriff nor the mayor took adequate measures to prevent a riot from erupting again, a mob unexpectedly gathered outside the Friends Shelter for Colored Orphans and attempted to burn that building as well. With help from respectable friends and neighbors, constable Morton McMichael, who later served as sheriff of Philadelphia during the 1844 riots, drove off rioters and permitted the firefighters to save the orphanage. The following morning, when the Philadelphia *Public Ledger* published an editorial condemning the cowardly attack on the orphanage, troops had to be brought to guard the paper's offices from a threatened attack.

The burning of Pennsylvania Hall notwithstanding, by the late 1830s the most violent phase of anti-abolitionism had passed. The Panic and Depression of 1837 cut deeply into contributions from sympathetic philanthropists, and abolition societies in the North and Midwest dramatically curtailed their efforts. In addition, northerners seemed to grow accustomed to the abolitionists' presence, and increasingly ignored them. Former opponents realized that the abolitionists were not going to bring the nation or the Constitution tumbling down, nor was the emancipation of large numbers of slaves likely to occur in the immediate future. Some even came to appreciate the degree to which the abolitionists were defenders of the constitutional right to free speech; the violent efforts needed to silence the anti-slavery forces seemed to many worse than the doctrines they were advocating. Finally, increasing numbers of northerners became disturbed by the southern argument, emerging in the late 1830s, that slaveowners had a right to carry their slaves into the Federal territories, such as Kansas and Nebraska, and turn them into slave states. Most northerners accepted the evil of slavery where it was—in the South—but wished to preserve the western territories as a place of opportunity for free white farmers, tradesmen, artisans, and investors. When the South denied the right of Congress or a territorial legislature to prohibit slavery in the federal territories, even anti-abolitionists began to see that the continued existence of slavery might impinge directly on their own economic aspirations. Thus the abolitionists earned a slow and grudging tolerance in the North. By the 1840s, most instances of collective violence revolved around ethnic and racial conflict rather than anti-abolition efforts.

# 4. *Expressive and Recreational Rioting*

Thus far, we have seen how preservatist groups used collective violence to impose their dominance on immigrants, Catholics, Mormons, blacks, and abolitionists. But Jacksonian era rioting also served other, less overtly political ends. Some groups, most notably vigilantes, volunteer firefighters, street gangs, community residents, and local political organizations, used collective violence to reinforce their own solidarity, or to communicate that solidarity to the outside world. This form of rioting, labeled *expressive* by sociologists, served a function similar to that of religious ceremonies, saints' day celebrations, July Fourth, Columbus Day, or other public holidays and festivities that demonstrate the cohesiveness of a particular ethnic, racial, social, national, or political group.

Jacksonian rioting also offered some urban groups a *recreational* outlet, a way for the young particularly to release the physical and emotional energies that arise naturally in all of us. Jacksonian cities offered their citizens few formal opportunities or facilities for recreation or sport, and so some rioting, particularly election riots, volunteer firemen's fights, and street-gang battles, took on the character of organized team sports. While the line between political violence and expressive or recreational violence should not be too sharply drawn, it seems clear that, unlike the riots described in the previous chapter, the violence we are about to examine was not intended by its participants to oppress or exploit an entire class or identifiable group of persons, nor was it intended primarily to further political goals. Instead, the riots described in this chapter functioned to support group or community solidarity, or simply to provide pleasure to their participants.

## Election Riots

Despite their seemingly political title, Jacksonian election riots occupied a twilight zone between political and recreational violence. While political campaigns provided the pretext for these outbreaks, it is not at all clear that most election riots had as their chief purpose the winning of elections. Just as often, the two sides seem to have fought as a way of settling ancient grudges, or of reinforcing their members' sense of commitment and solidarity. Even though the victors in an election riot did stand to gain votes, or more accurately, to deprive their opponents of votes in one or more election districts or wards, the object of a typical election riot was not to destroy the opposition party as a political organization. Election rioting did not usually have ideological content; the rioters did not fight to advance or defend political principles. Rather, they fought because it was entertaining, and because it was a way of preventing the other side from gaining votes. That votes in a Jacksonian election could be controlled through the use of violence was possible only because of the weakness of urban law enforcement in the pre-Civil War period, and because of the peculiar mechanics by which Jacksonian era elections were conducted.

The Jacksonian years were a time of highly partisan political loyalties, and most voters adhered strongly to Whig, Democratic, or American Republican principles. But ideologies were not the only force that
bound men to their parties. Group voting patterns in the Age of
Jackson often corresponded with ethnic, religious, economic, or social
characteristics. We can assume that since the Whigs and Democrats
differed relatively little on the major political issues of the day, groups
such as immigrants, Yankees, Catholics, or Protestants voted solidly
for one or the other party, at least in part, as much to reinforce their
own solidarity as to express political views. Bloc voting, then, demon-
strated a group's distinctiveness as well as its sense of competition
with other groups. Politics became one more way of identifying with
one's own group and dissociating from one's ethnic, religious, or social
rivals.

Within the violent context of Jacksonian cities, political rivalries
were easily translated into election rioting. Electoral campaigns were
commonly characterized by bitter personal attacks and aggressively
slanderous language. Ugly verbal assaults and even individual duels
were an accepted if not expected part of campaigning. The political
atmosphere of that day seemed quite heated and violent as compared
to the more polite standard of our own time.

That this turbulent spirit became violent in practice, however, was
due in large part to the mechanics of voting in pre-Civil War elections.
There were no laws providing for secret ballots and private voting
booths; party loyalists on both sides could crowd around the ballot
boxes, pressure voters, and clash with each other. In the larger cities it
was common for each ward or voting district to have a central polling
place, often in a favored tavern or hotel rather than in a municipal
building. The sale of alcohol at these polling places was rarely pro-
hibited and often encouraged. Contributing further to the turbulent
character of elections was the tradition in many cities of 'Lection Day,
a one- to three-day period during which the polls were held open for
voters. 'Lection Day was a time for politicking, entertaining, drinking,

celebrating, and brawling. The custom had begun in an earlier time, when most Americans lived in rural areas far from towns and needed an extended time period in which to reach a polling place. Even as the nation grew increasingly urban and election periods were reduced to a single day, the rowdy traditions of 'Lection Day, particularly the drinking and carousing, held on stubbornly.

Such conditions conspired to produce a steady stream of violence at election times. Concerning Pennsylvania elections, upper-class Philadelphian Sidney George Fisher complained that "a resort to brute force has now become familiar and expected." He observed during the presidential election of 1840 that

> Everything is done to keep up the excitement—meetings, speeches, processions are daily and hourly held and made and marched through the country. These numerous and constantly recurring elections are a growing and very serious evil. Their results are party spirit, bad passions, demagogism, idleness, drunkenness, mobs and riots. The people are kept in a constant state of agitation. The demon of democracy is abroad and triumphant and will drive us to the devil before long.[1]

While most Americans probably felt less threatened by election disorder than did Sidney George Fisher, many did recognize that violence at the polls influenced the fairness of the voting process. This was particularly true in cases where fighting and disorder were directly intended to guarantee victory for one side or the other. In Philadelphia as elsewhere, each of the political parties was known to have hired volunteer firefighters, street gangs, or professional thugs to serve as poll watchers, and these strong-arm types would block the opposition's voters from reaching the ballot box. Sometimes the rowdies

---

1. Sidney George Fisher, *A Philadelphia Perspective: The Diary of Sidney George Fisher, Covering the Years 1834-1871*, N. B. Wainwright, ed. (Philadelphia, 1967), p. 104.

would start a fight or a fire to create a diversion. In the ensuing
confusion they would steal the other side's ballot box or destroy it.
More than one election was won in New York, Boston, or Philadelphia
because a ballot box ended up at the bottom of a river.

The Moyamensing election riot of October 1834 was typical of the
political violence of the era. The Whigs of Moyamensing, at that time
in the majority, started a scuffle that prevented the district's Democrats from reaching the voting window. The Whigs grew so bold as to
smash some lights that the Democrats were using to illuminate their
banners. The fighting spread to the east side of Moyamensing Commissioners' Hall, where the Democrats had erected two tents and a
hickory pole. The Whigs drove their rivals away, tore down their tents,
and cut down the pole. Having driven the enemy from the field, the
Whigs celebrated their victory.

Their pleasure proved fleeting. Word spread to the Democratic
strongholds of Southwark and Northern Liberties that the Moyamensing Whigs had committed the sin of cutting down a Democratic hickory pole. Each neighborhood sent a delegation of its best fighters to
Moyamensing, and they converged on the Whig headquarters, a three-
story brick building located across from Commissioners' Hall. Like
their Democratic counterparts, the Whigs had erected a hickory pole
in front of their headquarters, only theirs was wrapped halfway up
with a metal casing to prevent mischiefmakers from trying to cut it
down. As the Democrats worked at leveling the pole, shots rang out
from Whig headquarters, and some fifteen or twenty Democratic supporters fell wounded, one of whom later died. The Democrats grew
furious and attacked the Whig headquarters. The occupants were
driven out and beaten, the windows broken, and the furniture tossed in
the street and used to start a bonfire around the hickory pole. The fire
soon spread to some adjoining houses, and when the firefighters
arrived to save the buildings, the crowd would not permit them to
approach. The buildings apparently belonged to a man with known
Whig loyalties, and they were left to burn to the ground.

Sometimes the passions of a political campaign merged with other social tensions of the era. An 1849 election riot—again in Moyamensing—turned into a racial disturbance of major proportions. On election day, local Democratic leaders employed a gang known as the Killers to serve as poll watchers. Bored by the lack of action at their polling place, the Killers picked a fight with some neighborhood Whigs. Having won that battle, they then turned the disturbance into a pretext for attacking the owner of the California House Hotel, who was a mulatto man married to a white woman. The Killers grew increasingly enthusiastic about their work, and after ripping up the hotel's furniture and scattering its inhabitants, they set the building on fire. They then continued to amuse themselves by declaring a "nigger hunt" in the black sections of Moyamensing, killing three blacks and leaving at least two dozen injured before troops finally arrived to restore order in the neighborhood.

Neither of the Moyamensing election riots seems to have had much *political* content, since the rioters were not fighting to uphold political principles nor to dismantle their rival as a political party. Neither Whigs nor Democrats believed that an election riot could literally drive the other party out of existence. But the Baltimore election riots of 1856–58 seem in fact to have had exactly this purpose in mind. The violence at Baltimore's municipal elections was started by the city's Know-Nothing organization, the successor to the American Republican party of the 1840s. Baltimore's Know-Nothings felt strongly that immigrants in particular and Democrats in general represented a clear threat to the existence of the American republic, and that these groups should be deprived of an opportunity to participate in the electoral process by which the city and nation were governed. Since neither the Congress nor the Maryland legislature would do anything to deprive immigrants of their right to vote, Baltimore's Know-Nothings instituted a reign of terror from 1856 to 1858 in an attempt to keep the city's immigrants, if not all Democratic voters, away from the polls.

Perhaps the worst outrages occurred during the presidential elections on November 4, 1856. At that time, Baltimore still used a system of one voting site per ward, and voters still handed in their paper ballots at a window. The Know-Nothings printed their ballots with distinctive blue-and-white stripes, and they pushed, punched, kicked, or stabbed with knives and shoemakers' awls (sharp picks used to punch holes in leather) any voters with unmarked ballots to keep them away from the voting window. In the Second and Eighth wards, some voters were killed outright. The Know-Nothings there simply attacked the voting places with battalions of men carrying muskets and pistols, and the Democrats retaliated by returning gunfire of their own. A historian of Baltimore described the scene picturesquely:

> The climax, however, was reached in the afternoon in the Sixth ward. Here the cannons were brought into play, and a pitched battle developed on Orleans street, near the Belair Market, between the Eighth Ward Democrats, who were called to the rescue of their comrades and who were the possessors of the cannon, and the Sixth and Seventh Ward Know-Nothings. At first driven back, but not to be outdone, the Know-Nothings brought forward and unlimbered a small swivel, and the battle raged, with varying fortunes, for several hours. The police finally secured the Democratic artillery; but those who had manned the latter succeeded in capturing and upsetting the Know-Nothing swivel gun, when darkness put an end to the combat. During the melee, windows were closed, houses were barred, and women and children sought safety from flying bullets in cellars and garrets. Notwithstanding this, it was astonishing how many boys were engaged in the fighting, and how many of these were shot while looking on.[2]

The Know-Nothing candidate for mayor, Thomas Swann, won the election, such as it was, by a margin of 9,000 votes.

---

2. Quotations in this and the following paragraph taken from Clayton Colman Hall, ed., *Baltimore: Its History and People* (New York, 1912), pp. 157, 158.

The campaign of 1857 was far calmer than that of 1856, primarily because most Democratic voters were afraid to vote. During the mayoral election of 1858, however, a coalition of native Democrats, peaceable ex-Whigs, and some Know-Nothings who disapproved of their party's strong-armed tactics organized a Reform party to contest the Swann machine. Mayor Swann himself was in charge of the police, whose job it was to protect voters at the polls, and of course he instructed his men to ignore any violence aimed at Reform voters. "Armed ruffians had complete charge of the polls, and it was as much as life was worth to attempt to cast any ballot but the Know-Nothing ticket." While there were no major riots or exchanges of gunfire, the Know-Nothings used their shoemakers' awls to injure and intimidate their opponents, and few attempted in any but the most solidly Democratic wards to vote. By late morning of election day, it was clear to the Reform candidate that he could not win under these conditions, and that his followers were indeed risking their lives to vote for his candidacy. He therefore withdrew from the contest at noon, issuing a statement condemning the Know-Nothings' tactics, and Mayor Swann was reelected by over 14,000 votes.

As a result of the turbulent elections of 1856 and 1858, the Democratically controlled Maryland legislature altered Baltimore's city charter, relinquishing control of the police from the mayor and giving it to a state-appointed board of commissioners instead. The Know-Nothings on the police force were removed, and in the election of 1860 the reformed police force was able to preserve peace. The Democrats, in fact, recaptured the mayor's office in the 1860 elections, and Baltimore's reign of political terror came to an end.

## *Economic and Labor Violence*

For American historians, the terms "economic violence" and "labor violence" usually call forth images from the Gilded Age of armed clashes between strikers and police, industrial sabotage, commodity riots, and the other trappings of open class warfare. Between 1877 and 1940, the United States had the bloodiest and most chaotic labor history of any nation in the industrialized West. During those years thousands if not hundreds of thousands of workers, police officers, private police, and National Guardsmen were killed or injured.

With some exceptions Jacksonian America escaped this fate. Prior to the 1850s there was little heavy industry in the United States: Only textile manufacturing, iron working, and steam locomotive construction were carried out in factories that employed at least two hundred persons. Most other Jacksonian workers toiled in smaller shops, or "manufactories," knew their employers personally, were respected for the level of their skills, and had not yet developed a sense of rigid class distinctions between employers and employees.There were some labor union leaders, such as William Heighton of Philadelphia, who spoke of irreconcilable class conflict between producers and capitalists, but most craft workers and artisans in Jacksonian America seem to have seen themselves as potential capitalists or potential master craftsmen rather than as permanent members of an exploited and oppressed proletariat.

Despite the ideological harmony between Jacksonian employers and employees, workers did organize craft unions whose function it was to raise wages and improve working conditions. These unions occasionally called strikes in pursuit of union goals; and these strikes caused occasional violence between employers and employees. Strikers sometimes fought against fellow workers, called scabs, who refused to honor their strikes, and against peacekeeping forces such as constables, sheriff's posses, or state militia. Such violence, of course, was overtly intended to force employers to give in to the strikers' demands. Just as important, it served to boost the strikers' solidarity and morale at a time when they were not working, not earning money, and rapidly consuming the meager savings that they had accumulated in the months or years before the strike. Let us look in detail at the Kensington Weavers' Strike of 1842-43 as a way of understanding how

Jacksonian labor and economic violence served to reinforce solidarity among urban working-class groups.

Philadelphia's handloom weavers were clustered in the city's industrial suburbs, particularly Kensington, Southwark, and Moyamensing. Unlike textile workers in Massachusetts or Rhode Island, they were not yet gathered into large spinning and weaving mills. Instead, Philadelphia's handloom weavers tended to work in small shops under the direction of a master weaver or in their own modest homes with their wives and children. Those who toiled at home usually contracted work with a merchant, master weaver, or employer who supplied the raw wool or cotton. Each individual weaver then spun the raw material into thread and wove it into cloth. The employer collected the finished goods and sold them in local or national markets. Weavers were paid on a piece-rate basis, that is, they were paid for each piece of cloth actually completed rather than by the day or the hour.

Ever since the Panic of 1837, Philadelphia's handloom weavers, many of whom were Irish immigrants or their children, had suffered from steady declines in their piecework rates. In 1842, the weavers' union tried to force employers to restore the piecework rates they had been paying before the depression, but the merchants and masters claimed that their slowly recovering profits could not yet support a wage increase. Employers insisted that a wage hike would drive up prices and make their products noncompetitive with those produced in New England's power-driven mills. Consequently, in the summer of 1842, organized handloom weavers struck in Kensington and Southwark, but employers had no difficulty in locating scab workers willing to weave at the prevailing rates. Many of these scabs were newly-arrived Irish immigrants with few alternative employment opportunities in the slumping Philadelphia economy and no ties to the handloom weavers' union.

Thus the strike pitted not only weavers against their masters and employers, but Irish countrymen against each other. It was from this latter conflict, the struggle of strikers and scabs, that most of the violence derived. In order to prevent scabs from working, strikers took to marching in the streets with signs and banners, shouting slogans, and entering the homes of scabbing weavers, smashing their looms, ruining their supplies of cotton or wool, and breaking their furniture. These actions served both to punish the victims and to intimidate any striking neighbors who might have considered scabbing. Outbreaks of these attacks continued through the fall and winter of 1842 and the spring of 1843. They culminated in a riotous confrontation at the Nanny Goat Market between the striking weavers and Sheriff Morton McMichael.

In January 1843, the weavers were holding a noisy demonstration and were about to leave on a scab-hunting expedition when McMichael and 150 of his deputies appeared on the scene. When the sheriff ordered the demonstrators to disperse, hundreds of shouting weavers pelted McMichael with paving stones and brickbats. All but two of his deputies immediately fled, leaving McMichael and his two stalwarts to be punched, kicked, and battered with flying objects. McMichael dragged himself away and called on the militia. They then occupied the neighborhood and arrested some of the demonstrators, who were busy celebrating their victory. Anti-scab violence continued until the strike was settled a few weeks later. For their efforts the unionized weavers won a small increase in their piece rates.

Aside from labor strikes, the Jacksonian era witnessed other forms of violent economic protest. For example, the neighborhood around the Nanny Goat Market produced yet another round of conflict in 1840, when residents of Front Street protested the construction of a railroad down the middle of their street. In March 1839, the Philadelphia and Trenton Railroad had convinced the state legislature to grant it permission to connect its Kensington and Northern Liberties terminals so that passengers and freight traveling between Philadelphia and New York would not have to detrain at one terminal and reboard two miles away at the other. Kensington neighborhood residents, unconcerned with the railroad's convenience, feared that its coal-spewing locomotives posed a fire hazard to their homes, that their children would be unsafe playing near the tracks, that their property values would decline if the noisy trains were running on the street, that wagon traffic, a staple of the Kensington economy, would be disrupted, and that the neighborhood's teamsters would lose the business created by the need to transfer goods and passengers between the two terminals.

The riotous opposition to the Philadelphia and Trenton's attempt to connect its terminals illustrates quite well the link in Jacksonian America between collective violence and other forms of political activity. When the railroad bill first came before the Pennsylvania legislature, it was clear that it had generated local opposition: All twenty delegates from Philadelphia county, Whigs and Democrats alike, voted against the bill. Yet the influence of the Philadelphia and Trenton, and the lure of railroad development in general, was such that the legislature voted the grant over the opposition of the Philadelphia delegation. The lawmakers did not reckon, however, with the dedication or courage of Kensington's anti-railroad partisans.

The ethnic, religious, and economic conflicts that were dividing Kensington in this period meant little in the face of the railroad menace, and the residents in the neighborhood around Front Street—natives and immigrants, employers and employees, Catholics and Protestants alike—united to resist the intrusion. They began their battle peaceably in the legal arena. Soon after the legislature granted the railroad its right-of-way, a group of Front Street property owners brought suit in a state appeals court to overturn the legislation. The court upheld the act's constitutionality, but the Kensington Board of Commissioners, the district's governing body, refused to grant a work permit to the Philadelphia and Trenton. The board justified its refusal on the grounds that the state had entrusted the district commissioners themselves with jurisdiction over the safety and maintenance of the public streets, and that the state could not pass this trust from duly-elected public officials to a private corporation. The commissioners and residents vowed to carry the battle to the Pennsylvania Supreme Court.

The railroad, meanwhile, took the lower court ruling as a signal to begin work regardless of the Kensington commissioners' resistance. In early March 1840, workmen appeared on Front Street with wagons full of rails and wooden ties. They dislodged the paving stones from the center of the street, dug a roadbed, and began laying track. Their actions caused constant unrest and commotion in the neighborhood, and on Monday morning, March 9th, as the Philadelphia *Public Ledger* put it, "matters took rather a turn for the worse." Residents of the entire neighborhood turned out to rid themselves of the railroad nuisance. With threats and an occasional brickbat, the crowd persuaded the workmen to leave. The paving stones "were [then] replaced very carefully by the riotous crowds." At 10 A.M., the Philadelphia and Trenton called on William Porter, sheriff of Philadelphia County and brother of Democratic Governor David R. Porter, to provide protection for its employees. The posse arrived and made some arrests, including one Hugh Lemon, a "property holder to a considerable extent in Kensington."[3] The workmen resumed, but the crowd was not intimidated by the posse. Once again they made working impossible for the construction crew, and the day ended as a stand-off.

On Tuesday, the following day, the workmen reappeared only to be met by the women and children of the neighborhood. Once again the crowd was successful in driving the work crews away. As the scandalized *Ledger* perceived events, "The female portion of the community take the most conspicuous and active part in the matter; with their frock sleeves rolled up, they deal about them as lustily as was ever done by the males at Donnybrook fair, and if their fists won't suffice, they resort to paving stones."

3. All quotations regarding the Kensington Anti-Railroad Riots taken from the Philadelphia *Public Ledger*, March 10, 11, 13, 1840; July 23, 28, 1849; June 24, 1841.

Wednesday passed quietly, but Thursday, March 12, brought renewed confrontations. Once again the workmen appeared and once more the gathering drove them off. A shipment of rails was peacefully diverted by a group of women from Front Street to a nearby marketplace where the company would be able to retrieve its property. The sheriff appeared in the afternoon with a considerable number of men, but they were routed by a barrage of brickbats and paving stones. After the posse's departure, the crowd tore up about a block and a half of rails and ties, the entire progress of the project to date. As before, the demonstrators refilled the roadbed and replaced the paving stones. That evening, the residents held a meeting at the Commissioners' Hall to discuss the railroad issue. Passions were obviously aroused by the speeches because the audience left the hall, marched to Front Street, gathered up the railroad ties left at the market, piled them into a bonfire, and burned them. The celebration lasted into the night.

That afternoon, after leaving Kensington, a ruffled Sheriff Porter obtained a court order deputizing all the citizens of Kensington and commanding them to come to his assistance in quelling the disturbances. He also issued an order to all the constables and watchmen of the district to report to him for service on Friday. When he appeared in Kensington that morning, however, rather than press the peace officers into the fray, he announced that the railroad corporation had decided not to resume work until the state supreme court heard the property owners' appeal. "The same announcement was made by the Sheriff to the assemblage in the vicinity of the road," observed the *Ledger,* "who received it with unmeasured applause, laughed at their triumph, and carried their dye sticks home."

So things stood until Wednesday, July 22, 1840, when the corporation decided to resume work. The supreme court of the commonwealth had ruled in the company's favor, and the railroad assumed that the question was now settled. Things started well on the twenty-second, as the workmen were not disturbed in their labors. That night, however, in what was clearly becoming a ritual, a large group of residents assembled, tore out the work, replaced the paving stones, piled the ties in the street, and burned them. "The entire woodwork was consumed amidst yells and ventings of anathema on the Railroad Company and the Legislature."

This act of incendiarism was only a prelude to the major battle of the Kensington anti-railroad war. On Monday, July 27, the workmen resumed their efforts and met with another round of resistance from the neighborhood. They retired to the tavern of Alexander Emery at the corner of Front and Phoenix streets. The tavern, it turned out, was leased to Emery by Joseph Naglee, who was none other than the president of the Philadelphia and Trenton Railroad. That afternoon the sheriff arrived with 118 deputies. He, too, retired to Emery's tavern, which became the posse's headquarters.

After a considerable delay, Deputy Sheriff Eleazer Hand and the posse accompanied a column of workmen to the construction site and ordered them to commence working. When a man and a woman were arrested for making inflammatory remarks, the crowd grew angry and attacked the posse with "ground apples," the loosened paving stones. The posse was driven off with several of its number seriously injured.

Later that night, a regrouped crowd turned its attention to Emery's tavern, which was a three-story building with a brick front and frame sides. Young boys battered the tavern door with stones. When it was smashed, a crowd dominated by boys and young men invaded the tavern. Several police officers and railroad employees fled, but Alexander Emery stayed to protect his premises with his sword. The crowd overcame him and drove him off. Someone brought a barrel filled with wood shavings to use as tinder, and the tavern was put to the torch. Fortunately, the building stood surrounded by vacant lots, so no other buildings were immediately threatened. When the volunteer fire-fighters arrived to extinguish the flames, the crowd stoned them until they abandoned their efforts. They remained, however, to prevent sparks from spreading to other buildings. During the events of the evening, the police were able to mark the names of several persons prominent in the rioting, but only two persons were actually arrested at the scene.

As the issue stood in this stalemate, Joseph Naglee reconsidered his position. His tavern had been burned and his tracks still were not laid. This high cost apparently convinced him to resign as president of the Philadelphia and Trenton. Seven months later, in February 1841, the new president, Benjamin F. Stockton, offered the Kensington Board of Commissioners $3,000 to defray the cost of culverting and repaving Front Street if the commissioners would allow the company to complete its work. The board tabled the offer, and the company interpreted this inconclusive action as a sign that resistance to the railroad might be weakening. They decided to test the mood of the neighborhood once more by commencing the project.

Clearly, hostile attitudes in the neighborhood had not diminished. When the workmen appeared on Front Street on the afternoon of February 4 and completed a small section of track, a large crowd gathered and the workmen voluntarily withdrew. That night, around 10 P.M., the usual ritual of destruction, street repair, piling the ties into a pyre, and setting a bonfire took place. According to the *Public Ledger,* the crowd celebrated around the fire through the night and did not disperse until early the following morning. Several weeks later, on March 25, this exact scene was repeated for the fourth time since the project was first undertaken a year earlier.

This was the last neighborhood attack on the railroad workers reported in the press. The company decided to appease the property owners on Front Street by offering to pay them individual damages for their lost property values. It also renewed its efforts to woo the commissioners of Kensington. The corporation even offered to pay damages to the commissioners of Northern Liberties for work it anticipated doing when the Front Street project reached that district. At a joint session of the Kensington and Northern Liberties commissioners, officials from the two districts decided to accept a $7,000 settlement. This outraged the residents of Front Street specifically and the voters of Kensington in general. On December 15, 1841, the Kensington commissioners met in special session to consider reneging on their previous vote. Board Chairman Thomas H. Brittain admitted

that he had been one of the commissioners who voted for the settlement, but he repented by proclaiming that he would yield, in keeping
with democratic practice, to the popular uproar and change his vote.
Others followed suit. When the final count was taken, the Kensington
commissioners voted to reject the Philadelphia and Trenton's offer by
a margin of 8–3. They then agreed to petition the state legislature once
again for repeal of the bill that had originally granted the railroad the
right-of-way down Front Street.

The campaign to obtain repeal in the legislature had actually begun
months earlier. The Philadelphia delegation to the state legislature
had nonpartisanly been lobbying for repeal within the halls of the
legislature itself, and in 1840 and 1841 they orchestrated a series of
public rallies in Philadelphia to generate support for their position.
The story of that political movement and the lobbying effort to
overturn the legislation is complex and interesting, but it carries us
beyond the subject of rioting as community action that we are con-
sidering here. Suffice it to say that the residents of Front Street forced
their district commissioners to reject the Philadelphia and Trenton's
settlement offer; they also rejected any personal settlement with the
corporation. They managed finally, through their elected representatives in the state legislature and a strong lobbying effort of their own,
to obtain a repeal of the railroad's grant in June 1842.

The ultimate triumph of the railroad resistance produced a wild
celebration along Front Street. On Monday night, June 20, the residents mounted a "grand illumination." Almost every Front Street
house from Cohocksink Creek to Oxford Street was decorated with
burning lights and candles, and many of the houses sported flowers
and banners. Two illuminated banners dominated the display, one
reading in part, "THE TRIUMPH OF RIGHT OVER MIGHT . . . NO MO-
NOPOLY . . . FREE PASSAGE TO ALL," and another proclaiming that
"THE CONSTITUTION PROTECTS THE PEOPLE IN THE USE OF THEIR
HIGHWAYS." By the *Ledger*'s account, "the street was thronged with
great crowds of persons of all ages and sexes during the evening," and
speeches were delivered from the roof of a temperance hall. The spirit

of celebration carried right through the night, for on Tuesday the flags were still waving and "the people were still rejoicing in their victory."

The point here is not simply that the Front Street community was able to defeat a railroad corporation in an age when municipalities and state legislatures were bending over backwards to encourage corporate and industrial development, although there is a charm to the David-and-Goliath aspect of the anti-railroad campaign. What should be stressed is the impact on the neighborhood residents of participation in community-action rioting and politics. The spirit of the battle and the ritual celebrations enabled the railroad's opponents to force a change of heart on the commissioners of Kensington, and even to persuade the legislature to repeal a perfectly legal grant to a private corporation. That same spirit also sustained the will of the street's property owners to resist the lure of hard cash from the Philadelphia and Trenton in exchange for abandoning their resistance to the tracks.

Baltimore experienced a somewhat different form of economic rioting in August 1835, when "considerable numbers of people, 'good, bad, and indifferent'" gathered to protest the slowness with which the insolvent Bank of Maryland was repaying its creditors. On the night of August 5, a crowd of 10,000 assembled in Baltimore's Monument Square to vent their feelings over the bank's inaction, but the evening produced little more than some random rock throwing. The next night, however, a crowd gathered in the square once more, this time sacking the house of one of the bank's partners. When the crowd tried to storm the home of another partner, Baltimore's mayor organized a guard of citizen volunteers to protect the house. After several volunteers were struck by flying stones, they asked the mayor for permission to arm themselves, which he granted. The guard opened fire on the crowd and five were killed, twenty were wounded. The next morning, the mayor announced to an enraged populace that the shooting was done "against my will and advice," and the guard's leaders thought it best to leave town. That night, the anti-bank crowds were left free to rampage, and they sacked the mayor's home and those of four of the bank's partners. Hundreds participated and thousands more cheered them on. The following morning, an elderly gentleman called a large meeting of concerned citizens, whom he organized into patrol forces. With that, "the destruction, which was still going on, immediately ceased, and the citizen patrols that guarded the city for well over a week met no opposition."[4] Federal troops were poised outside the city, but were not needed.

The anti-bank, anti-railroad, and labor riots we have examined here were clearly grounded in the protestors' sense of economic or social justice and their discontent with the power of specific employers, corporations, or economic elites. Yet it would be difficult to argue that these riots reflect an explicit or systematic class consciousness on the part of Jacksonian workers, or a deep-seated hostility to all corporations and capitalist enterprise. The Kensington weavers were simply demanding a livable piece rate for their labors; the residents of Front Street sought control of their own neighborhood; Baltimore's anti-bank rioters expressed their moral outrage over the apparent fraud that they detected in the Bank of Maryland's dealings. These movements left no permanent political mark on their cities, no permanent organization on which other groups of economic protestors could later build. Rather, these sporadic incidents of violence served to express the rioters' sense of moral disgust or their feeling that an injustice was being done in a specific instance by those in positions of privilege or power. Their collective violence gave concrete form to their attitudes, and helped create an instantaneous bond among the demonstrators. In that sense, whether or not the Kensington weavers had won their strike, or the Philadelphia and Trenton Railroad had built its tracks, the striking weavers and the anti-railroad protestors gave expression to their commitment and communicated to their opponents the strength in numbers that they felt.

4. David Grimsted, "Rioting in Its Jacksonian Setting," *American Historical Review* 77 (1972): 376–377.

## *Vigilante Movements and Movements in Support of Moral Values*

Jacksonian America produced no clearer example of the use of violence to cement community solidarity, express feelings of justice, and apply moral values than the intermittent vigilante and moral reform rioting that arose in rural regions and, on occasion, in the nation's cities and towns. Vigilantes usually operated without the legal sanction of a sheriff or other governmental authority, but they served nonetheless to enforce the law in places where no established peace-keeping machinery existed, or where the machinery was working ineffectively. Typically, we picture vigilantes chasing horse thieves and cattle rustlers across the Wyoming plains. In the Jacksonian era, however, vigilantism was not limited to the West; in fact, rural sections of the South and Southwest produced a large number of vigilante movements. Even northern cities, suffering from the in-adequacy of Jacksonian era law enforcement, produced vigilance com-mittees who took it upon themselves to restore law and order in their communities.

In many respects, these vigilance movements, both rural and urban, resembled characteristic anti-abolition mobs. First, they were usually composed of community leaders and men of "property and standing." Second, members saw themselves as guardians of civic order, the law, and public morality. In urban areas, vigilantes suppressed activities such as prostitution and gambling, either because public authorities felt legally powerless to do so, or because those officials were too corrupt to take action. Rural vigilante movements, by contrast, usually arose because the illegal activities of horse thieves or other felons were more than the regular sheriff, police, or constabulary could manage. In either setting, vigilantes would sometimes bring their captives to be tried and punished by the established judicial procedures, but frequently the vigilantes imposed their own trials and summary punishment. All too often, that punishment was death by lynching. Historian Richard Maxwell Brown has counted 88 lynchings across the nation in the decades before 1850, and another 105 in the 1850s alone.

The leaders of vigilantism, often respected and educated members of their communities, some of them lawyers trained in the due process of law, argued that their activities, if outside the law, were in keeping with the higher laws of civilization and the principles of democratic self-government. They saw themselves as enforcing community standards of decency or morality, even if their procedures did not adhere to the standards of due process of law. They believed that they were doing a job that the law *should* have done. Thus, in 1825, a crowd that included clergymen and other substantial citizens marched on the local whorehouses of Portland, Maine, drove the women and their patrons out, and wrecked the buildings. In 1835, the good people of Vicksburg, Mississippi, lynched some unfortunate professional gamblers who had taken up residence in their fair city. During the Baltimore Anti-Bank Riot of 1835, the same crowd that attacked the mayor's house stopped at the residence of Joseph Bossière and demanded that he surrender. A week before, Bossière had been accused of seducing a young woman against her will, and while the allegation was not legally proven, the crowd was determined to obtain higher justice. The historical documents do not tell us what happened to Bossière after he surrendered himself to the crowd, although we do know that the demonstrators did not murder him. More than likely, however, he was punished physically for his alleged moral transgressions.

Perhaps the most impressive—and political—vigilance movement in the pre-Civil War years was established in 1856, in San Francisco, California. From mid-May to mid-August of 1856, the San Francisco Vigilance Committee literally captured the elected government of the city. The committee was headed by the city's most important businessmen, who in their three months of de facto power, hanged four men, banished twenty-eight others from the city with a warning never to return, and expelled David Broderick, the leader of San Francisco's Democratic political machine. The Broderick organization had won political control of San Francisco five years earlier, using the methods made common by Tammany Hall and other Democratic political machines in the urban Northeast. Broderick's mostly Irish supporters employed ballot-box stuffing, violence, and vote-count manipulations to maintain their power. Two of Broderick's followers went so far as to assassinate his most outspoken enemies, a newspaper editor and a United States marshal. The newspaper editor had been calling for a vigilante movement to rid the city of the Broderick machine. He argued that only vigilance could end the fraud at the polls and lower the municipal tax rate by reducing corruption in government.

On May 14, 1856, the editor, James King of William, was shot by James P. Casey, a close associate of Broderick's. The next day, the city's business leaders formed the San Francisco Vigilance Committee. In a matter of days, the committee's ranks numbered 6,000 to 8,000 members (out of a total population of 50,000 in the city). Most of the members were native-born Americans in their twenties and thirties; almost none had Irish-sounding names. The committee was so well organized that it actually required written applications from members.

Casey and another accused murderer were hanged after a trial before an executive board of the Vigilance Committee. The same board exiled the twenty-eight Broderick supporters, and it even put Broderick himself on trial. Rumor had it that Broderick was to be hanged, but instead the committee chose simply to exile him. The committee continued to enforce law and order until the municipal elections of August 1856, at which time it formed a political organization known as the People's Party, which won the election in a landslide victory and retained elected power for another ten years. While most vigilante movements were neither as well organized nor as long-lived as the San Francisco movement, they too served as an alternative or a supplement to the official process of law enforcement, and had as their intent the creation or restitution of civic order in their city, town, or region.

## Recreational Rioting

As with the election riots discussed earlier, the many gang wars and volunteer firemen's fights in Jacksonian cities resembled organized team sports. To illustrate the recreational nature of this near-constant stream of urban collective violence, let us turn once again to the experience of Philadelphia in the 1830s and 1840s. Founded in colonial times at the urging of Benjamin Franklin, Philadelphia's volunteer fire companies had originally attracted members from the middle and upper classes. The fire companies, like the city's other voluntary and charitable associations, provided members with an opportunity for fellowship and a chance to contribute to the community's welfare. Sometime in the 1820s, however, the social composition of the fire companies changed. Increasingly, the older, more affluent members withdrew to their counting rooms, drawing rooms, and private clubs. The leadership of companies was left to local political bosses, to ethnic community leaders, or, finally, to the strongest or most energetic members of the street fighting gangs with which the fire companies became associated. The rank-and-file members of most companies were in their teens and early twenties, much as was the membership of the gangs. It was this youthful element of the fire companies that most needed opportunities for recreation and comradeship, and the gangs and fire companies, with their emphasis on physical activity, competition, danger, and excitement, earned the passionate loyalty of many of Philadelphia's action-seeking youths.

The "fire b'hoys" had a long established tradition of recreational fighting among themselves that pre-dated the withdrawal of the elite in the 1820s or the political and social conflicts of the 1830s and 1840s. Competition among the companies flowed naturally from the crude state of Jacksonian firefighting technology. The volunteer companies were staffed by young men who purchased and cared for their company's equipment. Each neighborhood helped support its own company or companies, while city or district governments supplied small sub-sidies. The firemen's machinery was quite simple: pumping engines and hose carriages that were pulled through the streets by the volun-teers themselves (horses were not employed by firefighters until after the Civil War, when they were used to pull the heavier steam-powered pumping engines). The volunteers had to be strong, skillful, and daring to negotiate a carriage quickly through Philadelphia's crowded, narrow streets. Races and fighting among the companies were a natural extension of the competitive pride that the volunteer firemen took in their equipment and personal courage.

In its nonviolent form, competition among the volunteers stemmed simply from the desire for glory. Great honor accrued to a company if it could race to the scene of a fire before others in the area. It was a matter of pride for a company to be the first to attach its hose to the nearest hydrant. The Philadelphia press often noted which company took the honors at a fire, and the firefighters of Southwark even awarded the most efficient company the much prized "fox's tail," a red, white, and blue cockade of feathers that was "transferred from one to the other, as they [were] successful in the contest." Members de-veloped such strong identification with the fortunes of their companies that one observer reportedly knew of a fireman who "worked better after a long sun and a race with the P——and had beaten her, but if his company was waxed, he could not work at all and had to lose a day."⁵

Fighting among the companies could erupt in any one of a number of situations. If two companies crossed paths on the way to a fire, one might try to slow the other by inserting a wrench in the spokes of the

5. Quoted in Bruce G. Laurie, "Fire Companies and Gangs in Southwark: The 1840s," *The Peoples of Philadelphia: A History of Ethnic Groups and Lower-Class Life, 1790–1940,* Allen F. Davis and Mark H. Haller, eds. (Phila-delphia, 1973), p. 77; quoted in Bruce G. Laurie, "'Nothing on Compulsion': Life Styles of Philadelphia Artisans, 1820–1850," *Labor History* 15 (Summer 1974): p. 349.

rival's wheels or by cutting its pull ropes. Some of the more aggressive companies might simply stop their race to do hand-to-hand combat until one of the contestants was driven from the field. Victorious companies were known to tip their opponent's carriages over or to deface them, occasionally stealing them for days at a time. Fighting might also erupt at the scene of a fire itself as two companies, arriving simultaneously, fought pitched battles over the right to be first at a hydrant. More than one Philadelphia structure burned while the firemen battled for the privilege of saving it.

Among at least a few of the companies, racing, fighting, and feuding—rather than putting out fires—became a chief preoccupation. To provide a pretext for racing and fighting, some volunteers sounded false alarms and even set fires. Sundays were an especially busy day for false alarms and incendiarism because that was the day young volunteers were free from work and other responsibilities. Some companies developed long-standing feuds that shattered the peace of a neighborhood for weeks at a time.

One such feud, between the Franklin Hose company and the Washington Engine company in December and January of 1842–43, saw the two companies stage fights, raids, ambushes, and assaults throughout the city. The blame for this fighting is impossible to assess, since both sides published long, self-righteous defenses of their own blamelessness. What seems clear from the conflicting versions is the following: The Franklin Hose and the Washington Engine companies, both located near the center of downtown, were at one time closely cooperating friends, but the quest for a reputation as the faster company did their friendship in. In early December of 1842, the two companies responded to an alarm in the northeast corner of the city. Since the Franklin Hose had only a small number of members on hand, it hitched its carriage to a passing furniture wagon belonging to one member. With the aid of the horse and driver, the Franklin was able to arrive first at the fire, passing the more numerously staffed Washington Engine on the way.

Apparently the Washy, as it was known, resented this tactic by the Franklin, although the two companies exchanged nothing more than words. But the seeds of resentment were sown and a few nights later, during the excitement of an election for state militia officers, a member of the Washington Engine picked a fight with the leader of the Franklin Hose. While members of each company restrained themselves, the two men fought it out alone. On Sunday, December 18, the two companies exchanged hostile words once again, and the following morning they staged their first major fight after a false alarm. The Franklin accused the Washington of having a suspiciously heavy turnout, while an apologist for the Washy claimed that the Franklin turned out between three hundred and four hundred men, six to eight times its normal complement of members. Both sides used their horns, wrenches, and brickbats as weapons, but neither was a clear-cut victor. From then on neither company went out without heavy reinforcements.

On Tuesday night, December 20, when the Franklins were returning from a fire, the Washingtons set up an ambush. The official spokesman of the Franklin Hose claimed that only one in five of the attackers was actually a member of the engine company; the rest must have been hangers-on and gang members. The following Sunday night, the Washingtons apparently set a false alarm and attacked the Franklins as they passed Callowhill and Broad streets in Spring Garden, now part of North Philadelphia. The notorious Dick Manly, a known criminal and a leader of a gang called the Killers, led several hundred of the attackers. The Franklins were forced to abandon their hose carriage in a shower of missiles. The pro-Washy crowd gleefully defaced the captured prize, and the Franklins could only swear revenge.

This they obtained the following day. Four hundred or so angry Franklin followers, by the count of a Washington Engine spokesman, stormed the engine house that morning. Repelled by the Washingtons the first two times, the Franklins finally overran the building on the third effort. They drove off the defenders, seized the engine, dragged it to the vicinity of their own headquarters, dismantled the engine, and threw its parts in a gravel pit. The Franklins' actions cost the Washingtons $2,500, and the city protection by one of its fire engines. The destruction of the Washingtons' engine, however, was not the only incident of its kind: In March 1844, an unknown group of raiders invaded the Good-Will Hose Company's headquarters, stole their engine, drove it to the outskirts of the city, and burned it.

It was to gain strength in numbers that the volunteer fire companies joined forces in the late 1830s with Philadelphia's fighting street gangs. At this time, the gangs were becoming increasingly identified with one or the other side in the city's heightening ethnic conflicts, or with the Whig, Democratic, or American Republican political parties. By the mid-1840s, firemen's fights became direct extensions of the ethnic warfare that had provoked the great Kensington and Southwark riots of 1844, and for the first time in Philadelphia history, guns became an expected part of firemen's battles. The fighting became a political as well as a public order problem, and the city and district governments tried vainly to abolish the companies or end their subsidies. Allied as they were with the bosses of the major political parties, the volunteers were able to prevent their legal extinction until 1871, when Philadelphia's city council finally established a municipal fire department and abolished the volunteer companies. In reality, this reform reflects not the decline of political strength among the companies but the effects of modern technology: The cost and complexity of the newly perfected steam-powered fire engines had rendered it impossible for most volunteer companies to purchase and maintain their own equipment, and they were relieved to see the city take over their firefighting responsibilities. Many of them remained intact as street gangs or political clubs.

While we have examined several categories of collective violence in this chapter and the previous one, it should be clear that the lines separating the various types of rioting in Jacksonian America cannot be so easily drawn. For one thing, most detailed accounts in the period seem to indicate a sort of recreational aspect to all forms of rioting. Only an hour before killing Elijah Lovejoy in a heated gun battle, for example, Alton's anti-abolitionists had gone about destroying his press, as one onlooker described it, "in a quiet sort of way" and "seemed to be happy while engaged in breaking it into pieces." A local paper reported that after the residents of Front Street, Kensington, successfully dispersed the Philadelphia and Trenton Railroad's construction workers, the neighborhood celebrated with all-night parades, bonfires, and carousing. A witness to a riot in 1843 observed that ". . . the mob of Cincinnati must have their annual festival—their Carnival, just as at stated periods the ancient Romans enjoyed the Saturnalia."[6]

Jacksonian riots seemed also to exhibit an expressive quality, that is, they helped to communicate the values of a group and reinforce its solidarity. The Moyamensing Irish who attacked the black temperance marchers, the Kensington weavers who routed the sheriff's posse, or the Vicksburg moralists who lynched local gamblers all probably felt a sense of mutual purpose and cohesion as a result of their actions. Collective violence served even the most politically motivated rioters as a means of expressing their feelings of anger, joy, fear, alienation, outrage, or solidarity. Jacksonian riots are linked by this common expressive function to each other and to those of other times.

But the categories of collective violence are bound by more than their mutual grounding in strong emotions. Rioting in Jacksonian America was functional (sociologists use the term "instrumental") as well as expressive; it achieved practical ends for the rioters even as it satisfied their urge for instant justice or released their pent-up feelings

6. Quoted in Leonard L. Richards, *"Gentlemen of Property and Standing": Anti-Abolition Mobs in Jacksonian America* (New York, 1970), p. 110; quoted in Grimsted, p. 385.

of rage. Thus when we look at the anti-abolitionist mobs of the 1830s, the nativist riots of the 1840s, and the vigilante movements of the 1850s, we find in them a common core. Each group of rioters tried to use extralegal violence to rid its community of what were believed to be dangerous, subversive, or criminal elements. Similarly, nativist riots against the influx of immigrants seem little different from the 1829 Cincinnati "Bucktown" riots against the influx of free Negroes from the South.

A further overlapping among the categories of riots stems from the fact that a riot often served more than one function. It is difficult to decide, for example, if nativists attacked Irish immigrants because they believed in a different religion or because the Irish were rivals for scarce jobs, housing, and public services. Moyamensing's Irish, in turn, attacked black temperance marchers to demonstrate their solidarity with the white race, but also to scare rival black laborers from the Moyamensing docks. In the late 1840s, firemen's fights had not fully lost their aspect as a team sport, yet they increasingly grew intertwined with the ethnic rivalry of the era. Gangs and fire companies increasingly identified themselves as Irish or nativist, Democrat or American Republican. It is characteristic of the 1840s that a newly formed company of firefighters should name itself the Schiffler Hose Company and a street gang should call itself the Schifflers, after the fallen nativist martyr of the Nanny Goat Market. Similarly, the California House Riot changed from an election brawl to a race riot when the Killers chose to expand their role as poll watchers into that of "nig hunters," a perverse form of recreation that the Moyamensing gang had been enjoying for several years.

The Jacksonian period was characterized by a great variety of collective violence and disorder, the purposes and nature of which vary greatly in some respects and overlap in others. We are left with the question, however, of why the Jacksonian years were comparatively so violent, and why some groups chose to settle their differences through riot rather than through other forms of social or political interaction.

Apparently, men (and women) fought because they believed in the righteousness of their cause and the wrongfulness of that of their opponents. But every age has its causes, every group its grievances, every individual his or her need to express beliefs and values. The next chapter will explore the sources of violence in Jacksonian America to determine why in that particular period violence was so commonly employed as a means to these ends.

# 5. *The Sources of Violence in Jacksonian America*

As we have seen in the preceding chapters, Jacksonian Americans put collective violence to a number of uses. Various groups employed rioting to provide recreation, to express anger and emotion, to intimidate political or economic rivals, to punish illegal or unpopular behavior, and to reinforce community solidarity. We must beware, however, of confusing the *uses* of violence with its *sources*. Violence was indeed a means by which Jacksonian groups achieved particular ends, but it was not the only means available to them. In every period of American history, social conflict has been conducted through electoral campaigns and legislative politics, through neighborhood segregation, through economic competition in the marketplace and at the job site, and even through athletic competition—professional boxing, with its ethnic and racial heroes such as John L. Sullivan, Joe Louis,

Rocky Marciano, and Muhammed Ali has provided a classic outlet for ethnic rivalry. Thus it seems fair to conclude that the existence of conflict between groups does not predetermine that they must use collective violence to settle their differences. Groups may choose violent conflict, but such behavior is not required.

The question of why groups choose to act violently toward one another has escaped definitive explanation by sociologists, anthropologists, psychologists, and others. Similarly, historians have not been able to explain with assurance why some periods of American history have been heavily marked by rioting and other periods by relative calm. For example, the years between the War of 1812 and the presidency of Andrew Jackson were known as the "Era of Good Feeling," and the decade of the 1950s was labeled the "Silent Generation." The 1950s were marked by an unpopular war in Korea and an awakening of the civil rights movement in the South, and either one might well have caused violent protest. Yet it was not until the 1960s that anti-war and civil rights protests led to rioting and confrontations between police and demonstrators. How, then, can we account for differences in the quantity of violence between one decade and another? Why was the Jacksonian era, in particular, so filled with violence, upheaval, and riot? What were the specific conditions of the 1830s and 1840s that gave rise to constant turbulence and disorder?

When the United States was passing through its violent ordeal of the 1960s, the nation's political and intellectual leaders announced that urban violence had become a full-fledged national crisis, thereby qualifying it for official study by presidential commissions. No less than four such commissions, the National Commission on Law Enforcement and the Administration of Justice (1965), the National Advisory Commission on Civil Disorders (1967), the National Commission on the Causes and Prevention of Violence (1968–69), and the National Commission on Campus Unrest (1970)—informed the citizens of the United States that they were, and had been from the first, a violent people. The public was offered a number of explanations from each of the major academic disciplines for its penchant to riot. Let us review some of the most widely held and frequently discussed theories of American collective violence that emerged from the 1960s, and see whether they help us to understand the specific sources of Jacksonian rioting.

## Psychological Theories

The ghetto uprisings of the 1960s convinced many observers that groups turn to collective violence when they experience a sense of frustration, deprivation, or blocked access to the rewards and comforts American society has to offer. Bottled up for too long, this theory asserts, the psychological frustration of oppressed groups creates inner tensions that explode into hostility, disorder, and violent uprisings. Indulgence in destruction and mayhem by such groups thus satisfies their psychological needs. At the same time, violence acts politically to "send a message" to dominant groups and classes, informing them that those who are excluded will no longer passively tolerate their inferior position. This "frustration-aggression syndrome," in short, forces the ruling class to deal with the dispossessed and disaffected.

Applied to the nation's black ghettos in the 1960s, or to the anti-war protestors reacting to the Nixon administration's 1970 military invasion of Cambodia, the frustration-aggression hypothesis seems to make good sense. It fails to explain, however, why in the later 1970s blacks, Chicanos, and other low-income groups, feeling perhaps just as frustrated, deprived, or blocked from power and wealth, have not continued to riot, loot, and destroy. What alterations in police power, social programs, or group consciousness have "cooled out" the nation's ghettos? The theory, in other words, does not tell us the circumstances under which frustration will be transformed into aggression, or tell us under what environmental conditions the oppressed or excluded will rise up in anger and actively relieve their internal psychological tensions through violence.

Nor does the frustration-aggression thesis tell us very much about the specific causes of Jacksonian violence. The vast majority of disorders in the years between 1820 and 1850 were inflicted by those in the middle and upper reaches of society upon groups socially or economically below them. The two most frequent forms of rioting, anti-abolition riots and anti-Negro riots, were often led by men whose dominant status in society was well established. When Utica's "gentlemen of property and standing" attacked the New York Anti-Slavery Convention, they did not feel frustrated by their inability to partake in the political and social processes by which the nation was controlled. In fact, four or five of their number held public office. Nor could the white, middle-class mobs who drove the black population out of Cincinnati, or who closed Prudence Crandall's school for black girls, be thought of as deprived or oppressed. Similarly, white slave owners who killed their slaves in the aftermath of Nat Turner's Rebellion cannot be thought of as "frustrated" or powerless in any conventional sense of the term. Even those rioters who functioned near the relative bottom of Jacksonian society, such as the immigrant Irish, were not more frustrated or deprived than the blacks or white nativist street-gang members with whom they battled. Indeed, even if we interpret Irish violence against blacks as a symptom of Irish frustration, we must still explain why the Irish did not channel their resulting aggression into attacking those who most often frustrated them: the white Protestants and nativists who insulted their religion and threatened their exercise of political rights.

There is another variant of the frustration-aggression theory that *might* apply to some instances of Jacksonian violence. The "status anxiety" theory argues that a relatively powerul group will attack, or "scapegoat," a relatively weaker group if the stronger group believes that the other threatens its status or prestige. Violence against weaker rivals relieves the dominant group's anxieties and, at the same time, demonstrates its continued social, political, or economic superiority. Thus Philadelphia's nativists attacked the Irish because the immigrants seemed a threat to native Protestant political power, economic privilege, and religious dominance. The Irish, in turn, attacked the black temperance marchers of Moyamensing as a way to reinforce their own sense of superiority over the district's black community.

Like the frustration-aggression theory, however, the status anxiety theory cannot account for many aspects of Jacksonian violence. For one thing, there has long been a degree of status fluidity in American society; some groups seem always to be rising while others are declining. And usually, these status changes have not bred violence. Groups such as German immigrants from 1840 to 1870, and Jewish immigrants between 1930 and 1960, rose at a relatively faster rate than did other ethnic minorities in the nation's past, yet suffered far less violence than did the Irish in the 1840s or the Italians at the turn of the twentieth century. Does this mean that only certain groups rather than rapidly rising groups in general are likely to become targets of other groups' status anxiety? Furthermore, even those groups, such as blacks, that seem to be the perennial victims of rival groups' status anxiety have been attacked during some periods and not others. Thus although the status anxiety hypothesis, like the frustration-aggression theory, seems logical on the surface, it cannot account for specific outbreaks of collective violence in Jacksonian society.

## *Historical and Cultural Theories*

Americans have long believed that this nation was conceived in and born out of violence. Historians, Hollywood scriptwriters, popular novelists, and others have portrayed the United States as a former frontier nation with a living frontier mentality. Americans insist on the right to own guns so that they can defend their homes with their personal arsenals. Wyatt Earp, Davy Crockett, Daniel Boone, George Custer, and Billy the Kid provide the mythic background to the contemporary reality of high murder rates, ghetto uprisings, political assassinations, police brutality, mass murders, and organized crime. In the 1960s, black leader H. Rap Brown summed up a widespread belief when he proclaimed that, "Violence is as American as cherry pie."

At first glance, the argument that violence is an American tradition seems reasonable enough. Since traditions are practices that one generation passes on to the next, the argument assumes that cultural institutions such as the family and schools somehow train the young to inherit a faith in and reliance on the practice of violence. Thus anti-abolition crowds should theoretically have been modeling their behavior after the example of the Boston Tea Party or the Stamp Act riots; nativists should have thought of themselves as defending their homeland by force of arms, just as their forefathers defended the newly established United States from the Redcoats and Hessians. Even if the lessons of collective violence are not literally passed from parent to child or from grandparent to grandchild, Americans must somehow communicate their belief in violence from one generation to the next.

To some degree, this view of American culture seems accurate. The widespread presence of guns in contemporary America is certainly a visible sign of our long-standing preoccupation with self-defense, aggression, machismo, and killing. Violence is definitely a staple on television and movie screens, and it dominates our popular fiction. At the same time, however, the use of violence either in politics or in interpersonal relations is widely and consistently discouraged by almost every social and educational institution, and the nation's political ideology condemns the introduction of violence into the political system. Schoolchildren are taught to respect the outcome of the democratic electoral process, and even the most flagrant violator of public law and human decency is afforded the protection of due process of law. The conflicting ideologies of lawful procedure and frontier action—the Perry Mason image versus the Lone Ranger image—seem constantly to war with each other.

The disjunction between a widespread belief in the processes of democratic politics and the desire of individuals and groups to operate according to the frontier myth marks every period of the nation's history. Nowhere is this ambivalence more apparent than in the behavior of Jacksonian urban elites. The Philadelphia "gentlemen of property and standing," for example, who applauded and perhaps participated in the burning of abolitionist Pennsylvania Hall were outraged five years later when the Kensington weavers mobbed sheriff William Porter during their 1843 strike. Very likely, some of these same gentlemen even volunteered for citizens' peacekeeping patrols or militia duty after nativist mobs burned St. Augustine's or St. Michael's church. In 1835, Boston's civic leaders laughed when a mob marched radical abolitionist William Lloyd Garrison through the city's streets with a rope around his neck, but a year earlier they called a public meeting to condemn the burning of a Catholic convent in Charlestown by a crowd of working-class nativists. In our not-too-distant past, some of those who most loudly condemned violent protests by anti-war protestors cheered heartily when those same protestors were attacked and beaten by flag-waving hard-hats in New York's Wall Street area. Thus while it is publicly condemned when employed by unpopular or outcast groups, collective violence is tacitly accepted and even encouraged when those in power use it against those same outcasts. The questions we must ask, then, are why, in the Jacksonian era as well as in other periods of the nation's history, are certain groups singled out as legitimate targets for violence, and why does the traditional cultural bias against the use of violence and force not apply to these victims?

Perhaps it would be more helpful to abandon the discussion of violence as a tradition and instead to conceive of collective violence as a practice that derives from another, more overarching tradition: popular democracy. The ideology of democracy and the practice of violence have been closely related since the founding of the American nation. American apologists for the revolution against British rule developed several principles (some of them borrowed from seventeenth-century English political theory) that justified the use of violence as a political tactic. Resistance to government tyranny, propounded by Jefferson, could be used by nativists to justify their attack on the militia companies guarding St. Philip's church in Southwark. The citizen's right to arm in self-defense, enshrined in the Constitution, might explain southern white willingness to lynch blacks, or a vigilante mob's instant justice for gamblers or horsethieves. The principle of "popular sovereignty"—the right of the people to govern themselves—and the related principle of majority rule were used by rioters to rationalize their attacks on abolitionists or other radical and minority spokespersons. Usually, the processes of legislation, law enforcement, or political bargaining have proven powerful enough to induce minorities either to conform or to remain silent although they may disagree with majority policies. At certain times, however, majorities have used extralegal violence or intimidation to compel acquiescence from weak or unpopular minorities, or to punish them for their beliefs or their behavior.

In sum, majorities in American history have tended to respect the law—and even to condemn violence and extralegal actions—when (and only when) the legal or electoral process has worked in their favor. When the law falls short of supplying a remedy for grievances, or when public authorities have seemed unable to control the behavior of unpopular minorities, legal authority has simply been bypassed in the name of popular sovereignty or majority will. The Altonians who killed Elijah Lovejoy believed that majority opinon justified the suppression of free speech. The vigilantes who lynched the Vicksburg gamblers placed community moral standards over due process of law.

Yet to describe collective violence as a supplement to other political processes or as an application of a traditional ideology does not mean that the violence itself is a respected cultural tradition. The use of violence has not been a venerated popular custom equal to, say, rooting for the underdog or singing the National Anthem at sporting events. Nor has America yet generated a home-grown ideology of violence in the intellectual tradition of Pareto, Bergson, and Fanon. Rather, it has spawned a sporadic *practice* of violence that derives from its ideology of popular, direct-action democracy. With the exception of the feud violence of Appalachia and portions of the western frontier, violence cannot be said to have risen to the status of self-conscious tradition in American culture.


## Biological and Ethological Theories

Other hypotheses offered to account for American collective violence are those derived from studies of animal behavior (ethology) and the application of those studies to human behavior. In the 1960s, such well-known etholgists as Konrad Lorenz and Robert Ardrey argued that man is, at bottom, little more than an upright ape, a predator who has been held in check over the past few thousand years by artificial and tenuous bands of civilization. Furthermore, since man's animal instincts lurk close to the surface, the fragile ties of civilized culture are easily torn, and men all too often revert to savagery and the killer instinct. Riot, murder, and mayhem, ethologists argue, are truly embedded in the genes of human beings, and the outbreak of such disorders is the consequence of genetic transmission. As Ardrey puts it:

> Man is a predator whose natural instinct is to kill with a weapon. The sudden addition of the enlarged [human] brain to the equipment of an armed, already successful predatory animal [the ape] created not only the human being but the human predicament.[1]

Ardrey goes on to explain that the human predicament—the tendency to engage in violence and warfare—stems from "territoriality," or the instinct of animal or human individuals, groups, or nations to defend their biological and environmental support systems through force. Although the human species has come out of caves and into civilization, and while mankind—unlike lower animals—possesses language and reason, the territorial imperative drives individuals,

1. Robert Ardrey, *African Genesis* (New York, 1967), p. 322.

groups, and nations toward violence and destruction. Biology, it seems, is more powerful than reason, instinct more powerful than learning.

Applied to particular forms of Jacksonian violence, the ethologists' argument for biologically programmed violent behavior seems to fit well. The territorial imperative explains the tendency of gangs and fire companies to fight over "turf"; the resistance of Front Street, Kensington, residents to the extension of the Philadelphia and Trenton Railroad; or the efforts by the Irish denizens of the Nanny Goat Market to "keep the damned natives out of our market place." Collective violence can be seen as ingrained, even instinctive and inevitable tribal reactions that derive from biologically encoded territorial instincts.

Despite the neatness of the ethological argument, there is strong evidence to show that intergroup collective violence cannot be understood by simplistic analogies from animal behavior. That is to say, while individuals may actually possess a "killer instinct" when faced with the threat of real danger, it seems more likely that fighting is *learned.* Some societies, such as African pygmies, never learn violent aggression. In fact, scientists have discovered over fifty so-called "primitive" peoples whose way of life does not include interpersonal or group violence. Violence is thus not instinctive in all peoples.

Ultimately, the ethological hypothesis would have to argue that Irish immigrants or native Protestants are encoded with a *collective* instinct to fight as a self-conscious ethnic group, race, or nation. If, as the ethologists suggest, the entire human species is programmed to commit violence, then the violence committed by Jacksonian anti-abolitionists, nativists, anti-Mormons, or Irish immigrants could as easily have been perpetrated by randomly collected individuals with no common identity or purpose. That this was not so indicates that more than a random biological instinct to fight was at work in stimulating some groups to choose violence as a means of expression or action. If we are to explain the sources of intergroup violence in Jacksonian America, then we must look to social interactions among specific groups, rather than to biological instinct.

## Sociological and Anthropological Theories

Part of the nation's unique past stems from its ethnic and racial heterogeneity. More than a hundred nationalities and all of the world's races live, in varying degrees of harmony, in the United States. Sociologists and anthropologists have developed two basic views of the impact that ethnocultural heterogeneity has had on American society. The somewhat older view, whose roots can be traced back as far as the eighteenth century, assumed that the ethnic, racial, and cultural groups constituting American society would become increasingly homogenized over time, and that a new race, *homo Americanus,* would emerge from the social "melting pot." This new race would be a combination of old and new, encompassing traditional Old World cultures and home-grown New World culture. Recently, however, social scientists have grown pessimistic about the power of the American melting pot. Ethnic, racial, and religious differences, observers note, continue to fragment American society, setting group against group in the struggle for autonomy, power, and political or economic advantage. The current resurgence of racial pride and ethnic politics, and the violent resistance of neighborhoods to school and housing integration, point to the continued vitality—and persistent disruptiveness—of cultural conflict in American society.

The history of American violence tends to support the view that the melting pot has not done its job. The majority of all collective violence in American history, and the overwhelming preponderance of it in the Jacksonian era, was composed of racial, ethnic, and religious rioting. Only in the twentieth century has labor and economic or political protest rioting come close to approaching the volume or intensity of racial and ethnic violence. Americans seem, now as in the Jacksonian era, to have difficulties finding ways to live peaceably with people of other races, colors, religions, or nationalities.

But again, a word of caution before we label ethnic and racial distinctions a source or a cause of violence in Jacksonian society. Biological, cultural, and nationality differences can and have been a source of social *conflict,* both in the United States and in other nations around the world. Brazil, for example, is a multiracial society of blacks, whites, and browns that has evolved a social ranking system based on color, with lighter skins generally more highly valued than dark skins. Yet Brazilian society in the twentieth century seems to have produced little collective violence that can be attributed to racial conflict. Similarly, the Soviet Union is a federation of more than a hundred nationality groups and cultures, with Great Russians at the top of the Soviet hierarchy and Asiatics at the bottom. The Soviet government has stirred resistance among minorities when it has attempted to replace their languages or religious practices. But, to the best of our knowledge, this cultural conflict has not led to widespread outbreaks of collective or ethnic violence.

If ethnic or racial conflict has produced violence in American history, it is not because such conflict is inherently violent. Other conditions must transform that conflict into violence. To understand why ethnic or racial conflict in the Jacksonian years become violent, we must look to specific conditions surrounding the events that transformed conflicts from bad feelings to physical actions.

What seems needed above all is a way to account for collective violence in Jacksonian America that finds its grounding in the historical conditions and events of the period itself. Arguments from human nature or general sociological laws cannot account for the particular forms of Jacksonian violence. Nor can they explain why the Jacksonian era was more violent than the decades preceding it. We must recognize, of course, that there are some constants in human behavior, such as aggression and territoriality, that seem to manifest themselves to some degree in every industrial society. But in order to identify the sources of collective violence in Jacksonian cities, we must specify the environmental circumstances and influences peculiar to that time that induced Jacksonians to use violence as a way of dealing with their conflicts. Our theory, in sum, must be a historical one. Too often, biological and sociological theories move from the observation of a few case studies directly to cosmic statements about human nature or human society. That the nations of Europe fought bloody religious wars in the sixteenth and seventeenth centuries, for example, does not predetermine that Philadelphia's Catholics and Protestants would riot in 1844, any more than it means that Philadelphians have a built-in biological tendency to fight religious wars. Both the religious wars of Europe and the religious wars of Philadelphia were fought in specific contexts and for specific reasons. The remainder of this chapter will attempt to define some of the conditions that permitted urban violence to flourish in Jacksonian America.

Earlier in this chapter we discussed some of the ways in which groups have invoked democratic ideology to justify their use of collective violence. Notions of popular sovereignty, majority rule, resistance to oppression, and the right to self-defense have, in fact, rationalized popular violence from colonial times down to the present. Most historians agree, however, that the Jacksonian years, more than any other period, probably created the most wide-spread popular democratic consciousness in the nation's history. The hindsight of a century and a half has since permitted historians to question whether the "Age of Jacksonian Democracy" was indeed so democratic in its treatment of blacks, Indians, women, and ethnic minorities. It seems fair to say nevertheless that, to a majority of native white Americans living through the 1820s, 1830s, and 1840s, the presidency of Andrew Jackson meant an end to predominance by "the rich, the well-born, and the able," and its replacement by the "Age of the Common Man."

In many respects the democratic reputation of Jacksonian democracy rested less on positive government action than it did on symbolic political gestures and posturing. Jacksonian ideologists proclaimed their abiding faith in the wisdom of the common folk and their distrust of formal institutions, written law, and legal procedures. Jackson himself was no great respecter of due process of law. In 1806, he killed a rival in a duel, knowing that popular opinion and local custom in his native Tennessee would protect him from prosecution.

As president, Jackson refused to enforce a Supreme Court ruling protecting the Cherokee Indians from illegal efforts by the Georgia state government to confiscate their tribal lands. On more than one occasion Jackson expressed his personal sympathy for anti-abolition and vigilante mobs, and commended his postmaster general for illegally forbidding abolitionist pamphlets to travel through the mail.

In such a national atmosphere, it is little wonder that such niceties as the legal rights of minorities and constitutional protection for the free expression of unpopular ideas should fall victim to direct action democracy—mob violence. Jacksonians saw neither courtroom procedures, political bargaining, nor conventional law enforcement techniques as adequate protection for community standards. There was a distinct need, they argued, for political majorities, or at least those who acted in their name, to insure that justice, rather than the all-too-slow due process of law, was applied to radicals, criminals, and those who threatened the social order. While vigilante mobs represent the purest Jacksonian expression of direct action democracy, anti-black, anti-abolition, anti-Mormon, and anti-immigrant mobs shared equally in this variant of majoritarian ideology. As a spokesman for an 1858 Indiana vigilante movement put it:

> We are believers in the doctrine of popular sovereignty; that the people of this country are the real sovereigns, and that whenever the laws, made by those to whom they have delegated their authority, are found inadequate to their protection, it is the right of the people to take the protection of their property into their own hands, and to deal with these villains according to their just desserts.[2]

The use of violence, it would appear, flowed from the people's duty—and their inherent right—to self-defense and the preservation of the common good.

2. Quoted in Richard Maxwell Brown, *Strain of Violence: Historical Studies of American Violence and Vigilantism* (New York, 1975), p. 95.

Democratic rationalizations for rioting carried far less weight, however, when they were invoked by outcast or marginal groups to justify their use of violence. Thus Boston's 1834 Broad Street Riot, in which Irish funeral marchers clashed with nativist volunteer firefighters, or the street wars among Philadelphia's gangs, or the burning of the Charlestown convent by "neighborhood truckmen" and other working-class nativists could not hope to enlist the support, or even the tolerance, of respectable elements in their communities. When a city's "disorderly elements" and "dangerous classes" invoked the doctrines of self-defense and direct action to defend their turf, jobs, or social prestige, they found little sympathy from sheriff's posses or militia companies. On the other hand, when the respectable classes themselves were actively engaged in vigilante or anti-abolition violence, the democratic rationale seemed to carry a great deal more weight. In sum, it all depended on whose self was being defended, or whose rights and liberties were being infringed on.

Two examples from the history of anti-black violence in Philadelphia will suffice to illustrate this distinction. In 1838, as we have already noted, a crowd of several thousand turbulent persons gathered outside abolitionist-built Pennsylvania Hall in response to rumors that blacks and whites were "promiscuously" mixing there. Neither the city's mayor nor the county sheriff did more than make perfunctory speeches to the crowd asking people to disperse. The sheriff even reminded the throng that Philadelphia had a tradition of not calling troops to handle its popular disturbances. Within minutes of his words the hall was blazing, and the volunteer firefighters who arrived at the scene did little more than hose down adjacent buildings to keep the fire from spreading. The next evening, encouraged by the apparent immunity to which anti-abolition crowds were entitled, a lower-class crowd tried to burn the Friends Shelter for Colored Orphans. This crowd, however, was repulsed by a group of respectable gentlemen. Four years later, in 1842, a crowd of combative Irish immigrants received similar treatment. When they attacked a parade of black temperance marchers in Moyamensing, a large posse was convened to protect the blacks, and when these volunteers proved inadequate, militia troops were called in.

It would be incorrect to think that Philadelphia's respectable whites felt greater sympathy for the city's black orphans or temperance organizations than for the abolitionists and "amalgamationists" who had built Pennsylvania Hall. It is doubtful that white racism in Philadelphia softened at any time before the Civil War. What seems to have mattered is that the attacks on the Friends Shelter and the temperance marchers were carried out by Irish immigrants, members of street gangs, and volunteer fire companies. Similarly, Baltimore's anti-bank mob was allowed to assault the accused adulterer Joseph Bossière and threaten to burn the house in which he was staying, but when the crowd leveled the same threats against the principal partners of the Bank of Maryland, or when they placed the mayor's own home under siege, the city's respectable gentlemen formed an armed volunteer guard that, under the pressure of events, shot and killed some rioters.

By itself, democratic ideology cannot account for the frequency of Jacksonian rioting. Even today, most Americans retain their faith in the common man and their belief in the rights of the majority. Yet rioting is not nearly as common in the 1970s as it was in the 1830s. Other conditions, specific to the Jacksonian era, must account for the tendency of certain groups to enlist violence as a tool for conducting social conflict.

One of the more important factors contributing to Jacksonian turbulence was the predisposition of particular groups to use riot as a method for achieving political or economic goals, or for expressing their solidarity against alien or competing groups. In this respect, the immigrant Irish, both Catholic and Protestant, come immediately to mind. Ever since the seventeenth century, when English armies led by Oliver Cromwell slaughtered millions of Irish peasants in the name of Anglican Protestantism, Irish Catholics have conducted psychological, political, and guerrilla warfare against their oppressive English rulers and Protestant Irish countrymen. The battle rages still in the streets of Londonderry, Northern Ireland. In the early nineteenth century, before Southern Ireland gained its independence from Britain, Catholics throughout Ireland were deprived of many of their political rights, their property rights, and the freedom to offer their children a Catholic education. In addition, Catholic peasants and sharecroppers paid exorbitant "rackrents" to their English and Protestant landlords. In retaliation, the Catholic peasantry engaged in a form of violent resistance known as "Whiteboyism." The Whiteboys, organized bands of nightriders, burned landlords' property, killed their livestock, and assassinated rent collectors, government tax collectors, and landlords and their families. Protestants, in turn, were accustomed to arming against attacks by their Catholic tenants and forcibly resisting their claims to legal, social, and economic justice.

Little wonder, then, that when Protestant nativism reared its head in Boston, New York, or Philadelphia, Irish Catholic immigrants were ready and willing to renew the hostilities that had been so much a part of life in their homeland. Similarly, Irish Protestants who came to the United States in search of economic opportunity were equally prepared for violent confrontations with Catholics in their adopted country. Both sides, still nursing memories of the other's aggressions, proved more than willing throughout the nineteenth century to engage in bloody battles on the streets of America's cities.

While the Irish were a particularly turbulent element in America's cities, we must not overlook the impact of migration, industrial development, and urban growth on the overall disorganization of social and moral systems in Jacksonian America. Rapid changes seem to have created groups who found expression for their angers, frustrations, and fears through violence. Contemporary observers reported an unprecedented growth of street gangs and fire companies in Jacksonian cities, and most often attributed this development to the decline of traditional institutions such as Sunday schools, apprenticeship programs, parental authority, and the pressure of community opinion. In neighborhoods that grew rapidly, youths found themselves looking for new identities, and street gangs and fire companies fulfilled this need. Gang observers in our own time have discovered that fighting and violence serves to reinforce the solidarity of gang members, particularly those who are confused or unhappy about their own identities. It seems likely that in the flux of population shifts and physical crowding that marked Jacksonian cities, violent gangs emerged in response to the social and psychological needs of disaffected youth.

Violence also became a tactic for pre-industrial workers seeking to control the conditions of their labor, and was even used to retard the introduction of industrial technology itself. Skilled native craftsmen looked on the introduction of factories and mass production techniques as direct threats to their economic security. Factory owners were introducing machines to weave textiles, finish shoes, and sew clothing in order to displace higher-paid craft workers with lower-paid, unskilled, and semi-skilled immigrants, women and children. Strikers seeking higher wages or better working conditions sometimes used violence against non-striking workers to halt production in an industry. Occasionally they used violence directly against factories. We can never know for certain how many cases there were of industrial sabotage before the Civil War, but we do know that during the weavers' strike of 1842–43, a group of Kensington handloom weavers mounted an attack on a water-powered mill in Manayunk, an industrial suburb about seven miles west of Philadelphia, because, according to one contemporary account, it "manufactured, by a much cheaper process, an article of cotton goods . . . hitherto . . . made by the handloom weavers."[3] The attack was averted when the mill owner was given advance notice, but the weavers who planned the attack were seen marching on the mill with pistols, rifles, torches and

3. Quoted in Michael Feldberg, *The Philadelphia Riots of 1844: A Study of Ethnic Conflict* (Westport, Conn., 1975), p. 36.

kindling. It seems clear that the weavers intended to burn the factory in the tradition of England's machine-breaking Luddites, who in the years from 1817 to 1819 broke harvesting machines and destroyed other farming equipment that threatened to mechanize agriculture at the cost of their jobs.

But what of our warning that explanations of Jacksonian violence must be grounded primarily in conditions specific to the Jacksonian period, rather than in conditions found equally in other, less riot-prone periods? Surely such phenomena as technological change, depression, unemployment, upward and downward social mobility, the influx of immigrants, relocation of migrants, and shortages of housing and public services have characterized the nation's cities in periods that were not so persistently plagued by collective violence. Between 1880 and 1900 alone, for example, Chicago absorbed more than *one million* additional residents, yet the city suffered only two major violent upheavals in those years: One was the explosion of an anarchist's bomb and a subsequent police riot, and the other was a week of rioting that grew out of a national railroad strike. Neither episode, it should be noted, was directly related to tensions caused by Chicago's own rapid growth. Similarly, technological change since World War II has caused more dislocation and unemployment than in the previous two centuries combined, but with the exception of the anti-war and civil rights protests of the 1960s, the past three decades have been relatively peaceful ones, certainly when compared to the three decades from the mid-1820s to the mid-1850s. How, then, can we find the source of Jacksonian violence in urbanization or technological change when these same forces have caused far less violence in other periods of the nation's history? Was there a particular characteristic of Jacksonian cities, one that distinguishes them from American cities that witnessed even more rapid physical change and greater social discontinuity, that can account for the frequent collective violence of the pre-Civil War years?

The answer appears to lie, above all, in the *absence* of an institution during the Jacksonian years that would later be a commonplace part of every major American city: paramilitary, preventive police departments. Backed by a system of national guardsmen, state militia, and federal troops, post-Civil War police were the single most important factor in the decline of urban disorder, insurrection, and collective violence. It is this decisive innovation in municipal peacekeeping that we will turn our attention to in the next chapter.

# 6. The Response to Violence

The volume of collective violence in the 1830s and 1840s reveals the degree to which Jacksonian cities were unprepared to deal with social disorder. While the nation's urban economic systems struggled to absorb thousands of immigrants, rural migrants, and free blacks, municipal governments proved even less well equipped to deal with the violence and disorder that accompanied this rapid expansion. In the pre-Civil War era, city governments suffered from a shortage of manpower to police their citizens effectively. For various reasons, the majority of urban residents was not yet ready to surrender to local governments the tax monies or the authority needed to repress disorder and anti-social behavior. Jacksonian Americans seemed to possess a certain fatalism about the inevitability of periodic rioting—

"intestine disorder," as it was known—and so cities and their residents simply learned to live with collective violence.

But neither the fatalistic outlook nor the weakness of public authorities was to survive the 1850s. By the eve of the Civil War, most of the nation's major cities had established preventive peacekeeping systems along lines still recognizable in today's urban police departments. With their introduction, collective disorder declined steadily in the 1850s and 1860s, and the 1870s was marked by a higher standard of urban public order than Jacksonians had ever imagined possible.

However dramatic their introduction, the police were not the only innovation that helped to pacify American cities by the time of the Civil War. By 1860, the northern industrial states had made public-school attendance compulsory for their youth. Public schools were meant to serve as nurseries for moral training and good citizenship. At the same time, the temperance movement stepped up its legal efforts to curb or eliminate liquor sales to the urban masses. In addition, having fought to a stalemate in the street, nativists and immigrants both channeled their competitive efforts into electoral politics, further diminishing the level of collective violence in the 1850s. Finally, other events such as the Mexican War of 1846–47 permitted a significant portion of America's urban street-fighting populations to vent their aggressive feelings on a common foreign foe, rather than each other. When reinforced by determined and street-wise police forces willing and able to carry out a mandate for civic order, these developments helped to make the 1850s a far less violent period than the 1830s and 1840s.

Americans, it seems, have preferred to attack their social or political problems by legislating them away. Even in the Jacksonian period, civic leaders looked to the law as a tool for eliminating the negative effects of rapid change and the conflicts arising from cultural incompatibilities among the nation's ethnic and racial groups. As cultural diversity and racial heterogeneity increasingly came to characterize

Jacksonian cities, legislators, opinion leaders, civic reformers, and activists increasingly relied on the passage and enforcement of laws to restore the failing dominance of white Protestant culture.

One of the most enduring achievements to emerge from this legal effort to suppress the diverse cultures of the "lower orders" and integrate the immigrant masses into the mainstream of the so-called Protestant ethic was the passage of compulsory school attendance laws. By the 1840s, states with urban and industrial centers, such as Massachusetts, Pennsylvania, and New York, required that their youthful populations attend tax-supported public grammar schools. The public schools were intended, of course, to transmit literacy and reasoning skills that would prepare graduates for good citizenship and economic opportunities. In this sense, then, public education in the United States can be seen as a democratic device for leveling distinctions between the rich and the poor. From the first, American public education has been viewed this way. Less widely acknowledged, however, is the origin of public education in the context of—and as a remedy for—urban disorder. Pre-Civil War educational reformers hoped to use the public schools as civilizing agencies, places where children from the so-called dangerous classes could unlearn their parents' values and those of neighborhood social institutions such as street gangs, taverns, and the Catholic church. By no coincidence, in the pre-Civil War period and throughout the nineteenth century, a majority of public-school teachers were white Protestants, and school curricula stressed conventional Protestant morality taught in the guise of reading and writing skills.

It was this same "reform" and "civilizing" impulse, working to transform the schools, that produced the Jacksonian nativist and temperance movements. Like temperance, the schools were to provide "moral policing," more specifically, an internalized adherence by individuals to the values of sobriety, reliability, punctuality, neatness, thrift, and respect for authority. Such attitudes were essential to a society that valued capital accumulation and productivity, and highly useful to a society attempting to control the disorderly and violent behavior of its most turbulent citizens. Like nativists, who distrusted and demeaned the cultural values of immigrant Catholics, many of those who advocated compulsory public schooling believed in the necessity or replacing working-class and immigrant customs such as drinking and fighting with an ethic of self-control and self-denial. Thus the Philadelphia school Bible controversy, which combined nativist distrust of Catholic intentions with school reformers' concerns that the schools become agencies for teaching moral virtues, produced such heated conflict. At stake was the definition of American culture: If the "reformers" won, then Protestant hegemony was saved; if Catholics won, the United States was to have a pluralistic culture.

Just as the public schools were supposed to turn urban youth away from turbulence, destructiveness, and disorder, so too the temperance movement was expected to improve the moral climate of Jacksonian cities. By the late 1840s, temperance movements in New York, Boston, and Philadelphia had completed their transformation into legal prohibition movements. Prohibitionists developed two strategies for using the legal system to further their cause. First, they pressured their state and local legislators to enact laws prohibiting the sale of alcohol on the Sabbath, or in all but a few licensed travelers' hotels, or in units smaller than ten gallons. Second, in places such as Boston and Philadelphia where such laws already existed but were rarely if ever enforced, prohibitionists launched concerted efforts to force magistrates to shut down unlicensed taverns and to eliminate the sale of liquor in small units. The prohibitionists were often allied with Sabbatarians, who had been fighting for laws to prohibit the disturbing of church services, to end the delivery of Sunday mail, and to suppress various forms of popular amusement. In Philadelphia, for example, Sabbatarians proposed that on Sundays public officials chain off streets on which church services were being conducted so that the volunteer firefighters would not disturb the worshipers with their racing and fighting.

The effort to achieve moral and social reform through restrictive laws could not succeed, of course, if the laws themselves could not be enforced. In cities where colonial or eighteenth-century ordinances prohibiting Sunday tavern openings or small-unit liquor sales were still on the books, local officials already possessed the necessary legal powers to carry them out. Yet, over the years, they had let such laws and ordinances become dead letters, and before the rise of prohibitionist sentiment in the 1840s, few elected officials had the political motivation to see that they were enforced. But moral reformers wanted to guarantee that the laws would be enforced, so they moved to create new enforcement systems with the political will and sufficient manpower to get the job done. Those systems were to evolve into modern municipal police departments.

Undoubtedly, the two greatest spurs to the creation of police departments in the pre-Civil War period were, first, the rioting and disorder that plagued Jacksonian cities, and, second, the desire of moral reformers to enforce legislation regulating drinking, Sunday amusements, and school attendance. The sizable incidence of individual criminality during this era only tangentially influenced the creation of such police agencies.

Despite near-universal concern for reducing the collective violence that plagued Jacksonian cities, there was significant resistance to the introduction of modern, preventive police forces in the years before the Civil War. Various traditions and attitudes militated against the simple imposition of police forces on Jacksonian Americans. For one thing, many individuals were convinced that a certain amount of "intestine disorder" was not only inevitable but, in manageable amounts, healthy for the body politic. Even the revered Jefferson had suggested that citizens should not be so concerned with domestic tranquility and order that they surrender their liberty to a repressive government. Authorities capable of crushing popular disturbances were also capable of suppressing political dissent, popular participation in government—perhaps even freedom itself. Americans had already seen what strong police powers could lead to: the British occupation of the American colonies in the 1760s and 1770s, and the political repression imposed by Napoleon's secret police in the later years of the French Revolution. These lessons had bred in Americans a distrust of "standing armies" and other varieties of uniformed military or paramilitary peacekeeping. While Americans wanted their cities to become more orderly, many of them feared the potentially tyrannical instruments of government that would concomitantly be created.

It seemed clear by the mid-1840s, however, that some change in the system of municipal peacekeeping was inevitable. The systems then in use in Philadelphia, New York, and Boston, as well as in smaller cities such as Cincinnati, San Francisco, and New Orleans, were simply inadequate for maintaining ordered liberty. Whatever the risks to political freedom that might come from a "standing army" of munici-pal police, the existing risks to free speech, property, life, and limb seemed far more immediate and compelling. A police system had to be found that would preserve the basic freedoms of the populace, while still suppressing physical threats to law-abiding and peaceable citizens as they went about their daily business.

Before the introduction of police reforms in the late 1840s and 1850s, public order in Jacksonian cities was preserved by men who were neither full-time officers nor deeply committed to keeping the peace. Responsibility for law enforcement, public safety, and public health was assigned by day to elected sheriffs, constables, aldermen, or marshals and by night to politically appointed nightwatchmen, a system first invented in the Middle Ages. Many nightwatchmen literally "moonlighted," that is, worked—or just as often slept—on their posts, after putting in a full day at another job. Often, these men took watchmen's positions only to supplement their income. The rest tended to be older men, no longer able to earn their keep through physical labor, yet without other means of support. To get a watch-man's job, one's physical strength or ability to perform responsibly was less important than one's willingness to work for the political party in power, or one's personal connections with an elected official.

The typical Jacksonian nightwatchman, like his medieval counterpart, was the butt of pranks, jokes, and insults. Because they were armed with nothing more than a rattle with which to summon fellow officers in an emergency, the watchmen tended to huddle together for warmth and safety in their watch houses, some of which were not much bigger than today's telephone booths. Occasionally the watchmen would sally forth on patrol, looking for drunks to escort home, fires that needed extinguishing, or thieves who were prowling in the dark. Most of the time, however, they stayed in their watch houses, either peering out from inside or sleeping. It became a sport for city youths, both working class and upper class, to sneak up quietly behind a watch house and tip it over with the sleeping occupants inside. If the watchmen did try to make an occasional arrest of gang members, drunken rowdies, or criminals, they would very often have to fight the arrestee's friends to keep them from freeing him. Generally speaking, the system was quite inefficient and the watchmen's rewards for diligence few. Little surprise, then, that the night watch was inadequate to the task of peacekeeping. The system's one virtue was that it was inexpensive—for taxpayers, not for the victims of criminals and rioters.

The elected daytime constables (I will use the term "constables" to signify sheriffs, aldermen, and marshals as well) were only slightly more effective as a deterrent to crime and violence than nightwatchmen. In Jacksonian cities the constabulary system was highly democratic: The citizens of each ward, precinct, or district got to elect one or two constables who took responsibility for neighborhood law enforcement and who served as justices of the peace, that is, judges for petty offenses. Yet these activities constituted neither the constable's primary interest nor his primary responsibility. The bulk of a constable's duties revolved around serving legal papers such as court orders, debt collections, and mortgage foreclosures. Whatever money constables earned in office came from the fees they charged for serving these papers rather than from peacekeeping or law enforcement. Consequently, the constables did not patrol the streets seeking out crime or disturbances; if a constable was needed in an emergency, he had to be summoned from his office, workshop, or home. The fact that they were unpaid for preventing crime or keeping the peace explains why constables felt little incentive to risk their lives or limbs in defense of public order.

The constabulary's reluctance to get involved in public disturbances became most pronounced when the victims of crime or disorder were unpopular minorities. Few constables would risk their reelection chances by trying to protect abolitionists, blacks, Mormons, or other social outcasts from the righteous indignation of their constituents. Given that they were paid little if anything to protect these minorities, and given that their position in the community would be jeopardized if they did protect them, it is little wonder that, for example, Philadelphia's mayor, sheriff, and other law enforcement officials stood by at the burning of Pennsylvania Hall or during the sacking of Third Ward, Kensington. By extension, it is only slightly more surprising that, in 1834, Philadelphia Mayor John Swift *led* a mob that threw abolitionist mail into the Delaware River, or that one of those arrested in the Kensington anti-railroad riots was a local alderman who chose to participate on the side of his neighbors rather than to fulfill his obligation to protect the railroad workers from the rioters.

The worst aspects of Jacksonian peacekeeping were most glaringly apparent during crises such as the Philadelphia riots of 1844. To begin with, it fell to constables or nightwatchmen, and in major cities the mayor, to disperse crowds and prevent violence. Unarmed, unenthusiastic, untrained, and unpaid, these officials were least likely to act decisively to contain crowds and keep them from turning into rioters. Once a situation had gotten beyond the control of the local watch or constabulary, there were but two ways for public authorities to react. The first was for a mayor or county sheriff to organize citizen volunteers into a posse or peacekeeping patrols. Like the constabulary, these volunteers were usually unarmed and unlikely to have a stomach for confronting an enraged crowd of their friends, neighbors, or fellow citizens. On the few occasions when citizen volunteers were armed and willing to confront crowds, the results resembled those of the Baltimore anti-bank riots: The volunteers shot and killed some rioters, further angering the crowd and raising its thirst for revenge. The second and final line of defense became state militias, who also were composed of volunteers. These part-time soldiers, however, possessed a semblance of military discipline, were heavily armed, and were often brought from other parts of the state so that they would not have to confront neighbors or friends if deadly force was required. As a result, militias suffered two distinct disadvantages as a method of crowd control: They took too long to be gathered and brought to the scene of a riot—by the time they arrived, the rioting was usually well out of hand; and, since they were armed, their appearance often provoked shooting and the loss of life.

Most observers who reflected on the problem of Jacksonian violence agreed that a new system had to be found for *preventing* the outbreaks of riots, or at least confining disturbances and gatherings before they grew into major uprisings. Even enemies of standing police forces were willing to concede that, in theory at least, a civilian-controlled police, insulated from political manipulation, and using a *patrol strategy* to locate and isolate disturbances before they grew into riots, was far preferable to the chaos that had come to characterize Jacksonian cities. It was this patrol function that was to differentiate the new police from the old constabulary, and which accounts for the effectiveness of the police in maintaining public order.

In their search for a new model of municipal peacekeeping, Americans needed only to look as far as England, where in 1829, responding to much the same riotousness that was common in Jacksonian cities, the British Parliament had established the London Metropolitan Police. Nicknamed "bobbies" after their chief sponsor, Prime Minister

Robert Peel, London's Metropolitans were proving the value of a "preventive police" in controlling disorders with a minimum of physical injury. The London police were recruited as full-time professionals who were permitted to hold no other jobs and were expected to remain sober, honest, and diligent. Officers were allowed no role in politics, and until the 1880s, in fact, could not even vote in elections. Unlike American constables and nightwatchmen, the bobbies wore distinctive uniforms that made them visible to the public— to both those seeking help and those contemplating misdeeds. To increase their familiarity with the people they policed, London officers were assigned a regular beat and were required to live in the neighborhoods they patrolled. Disciplinary standards were quite high in the Metropolitan Police Force, and in the first few years as many as one third of the recruits were dismissed annually for violating the department's code of conduct.

Londoners had been as wary as Americans of standing armies and police forces on their streets. Before the Metropolitans were created, the British government had used troops and volunteers (called yeomanry) to suppress crowds and political dissenters, and these "forces of order" had done bloody work breaking up political demonstrations and disturbances. The government had also developed a system of spies to keep track of political dissidents. Little wonder, then, that the British public, especially the more liberal and radical political elements, feared that the new police would become an extension of the Crown's system of political suppression, intrigue, and brutality.

Faced by these public doubts, the early administrators of the Metropolitan Police, particularly attorney Richard Mayne, firmly insisted that the London police respect the legal and traditional rights of free speech and free assembly that were part of the English constitution. Mayne and his co-administrator, Sir Charles Rowan, also realized the importance of keeping the Metropolitan Police from interfering in the personal pleasures of the London populace, notably their drinking habits, sexual preferences, and traditional popular entertainments.

Thus Rowan and Mayne opposed the passage of laws prohibiting liquor sales or entertainment on the Sabbath on the ground that the effort to enforce such laws would serve only to create hostility between the police and the people.

Inspired by the ability of London's Metropolitan Police to reduce the number and severity of London's riots, American civic leaders proposed similar systems for their own cities. Despite their efforts, however, opponents managed to block major police reforms. It was not until 1854, a full decade after the devastating Native American Riots, that Philadelphia's city council was able to abolish the night watch system and reduce the constabulary to serving papers and hearing petty criminal cases. In their place the council appointed a full-time, preventive police department to patrol the city's streets.

Before 1854, a coalition of constables, aldermen, marshals, and local political bosses had used their political muscle to block the formation of a police department. These public servants feared, of course, that they would lose their political influence and powers, and that district political machines would be deprived of a major source of patronage positions on the night watch. Many of their constituents, especially in Philadelphia's immigrant and industrial suburbs, regarded a citywide preventive police department as a threat to their life-styles and personal interests. A centralized police department, they believed, was likely to be controlled by Philadelphia's Whig elite or the city's nativist political movement. The new police force would most likely be used to close unlicensed drinking places and Sunday amusements in working-class and immigrant neighborhoods. Ironically, some *pro*-temperance and nativist Philadelphians from "respectable" neighborhoods feared, by contrast, that the Democrats and Irish would gain control of a centralized police force, thereby blocking local enforcement of the very laws and ordinances they were struggling to obtain in the state legislature. Thus both factions preferred to continue the status quo. Finally, opposition to a salaried, full-time municipal police department came from taxpayers, rich and poor alike, who feared that the cost of such a force would be far higher than that of the existing constabulary and watch.

Yet the continuing pressures of urban upheaval and memories of the traumatic 1844 riots undermined local resistance to a Philadelphia-wide police force. By stages, the Pennsylvania state legislature amended the city's charter to create a recognizably modern preventive police department. In 1850, the legislature authorized the formation of a daytime "Marshal's Police," which was to replace the sheriff's posse and constabulary. The Marshal's Police were given jurisdiction throughout Philadelphia county and did not have to respect district boundaries. The chief marshal was elected by popular vote, but he was free to appoint officers of his own choosing. Finally, in 1854, as part of the consolidation of Philadelphia county's twenty-three districts, towns, and townships into a single City of Philadelphia, the night watch was abolished and the modern Philadelphia Police Department created. The marshal's office was abolished, and the mayor of consolidated Philadelphia was given the right to appoint his own police chief and members of the force. Philadelphia, in short, had adopted the typical contemporary form of police management. Eli Kirk Price, a wealthy businessman who steered the consolidation bill through the state legislature, later recalled that his fellow downtown Whigs dropped their opposition to the cost of a preventive police force when they became certain that they had the political muscle to control the new department and use it to harass unlicensed liquor sellers in the surrounding districts.

Similar relationships between the formation of the police and ethnic and cultural politics also applied in Boston and New York. The New York Police Department was formed in 1845, the same year that city Democrats regained political control from a short-lived American Republican administration. William Harper, the American Republican mayor in 1844, had formed a "mayor's police" during his year in office, abolishing the night watch and making the entire department accountable to his hand-picked chief of police. The force hired "none

but native Americans," but when Harper and his party were swept
from office their successors abolished the mayor's police and built a
new department with Irish and German as well as native-born officers.
In 1857, when the Republican party gained the upper hand in the New
York state legislature, it moved to wrest political control of the police
from the city's Democratic machine. The Republican legislature, supported by a Republican governor, amended the city's charter to abolish
the New York Police Department and substitute in its place a state-
controlled Metropolitan Police Force under the leadership of state-
appointed commissioners. Democratic Mayor Fernando Wood refused
to dismantle the New York Police Department, and when the Metropolitans appeared on the city's streets in their state-supplied uniforms,
the mayor instructed his constituents to disregard them on the grounds
that the Metropolitans were illegally invading the sovereignty of New
York City. The two forces coexisted for a time, but relations soon
broke down between them. The Metropolitan commissioners moved
to have Mayor Wood arrested for contempt of their authority, and the
city was treated to the spectacle of the regular police defeating the Metropolitans in a pitched battle on the steps of City Hall. Under the
shadow of a state court injunction, Wood eventually dismantled the
New York Police Department, and the Metropolitans took charge of
the city's law enforcement.

By the eve of the Civil War, there was greater acceptance of centralized, uniformed, preventive police forces patrolling the streets of
America's cities. In the late 1840s and early 1850s, however, their
reception, if not as negative as that of the New York Metropolitans,
was grudging at best. Symbolically, the officers' uniforms became the
focus of resistance to the authority of the newly formed departments.
When the first policemen appeared on the streets of Moyamensing,
one of Philadelphia's industrial districts, a crowd gathered and attacked
the officers and destroyed the district station house. Volunteer firefighters often harassed the officers, as did members of street gangs.
Some officers refused to appear in their uniforms, claiming that they

found them "undemocratic," but more likely fearing that the uniform made them visible targets for toughs who had formerly made sport of the watchmen and constables. But the police, even in uniform, survived their early baptism under fire, and most city residents came to have a feeling of ease because a uniformed, preventive police was guarding them and their property from attack or disaster. Like their London counterparts, the American municipal police grew in public esteem as they increased in usefulness, kept the peace effectively, and avoided offending a majority of citizens. America's early urban police forces won their final acceptance in 1863, when during the dark days of the Civil War, they fought to control the bloody Draft Riots that tore through New York and Boston and took more than a thousand lives in New York alone. While they required help from federal troops in suppressing these riots, the New York Police Department earned both self-respect and the grudging admiration of the city's residents for their courage in confronting the anti-draft rioters at the risk of their lives.

This is not to say, though, that there were more similarities than differences between the American and English versions of nineteenth-century police. Perhaps the major difference was the role that politics played in American policing when compared to the relative non-political nature of the London force. Appointment to American police departments was strictly political, just as it had been in the days of the constabulary and night watch. When the Democrats were in office, patrolmen were loyal Democrats. If the Democrats lost, the Whigs or American Republicans would bring in their own cast of officers. In no branch of government more than the municipal police did the old political motto "To the victor goes the spoils" so thoroughly apply. Police precincts were established on a ward or district level, and the local political leader or alderman of each ward was free to appoint his choice of candidates to serve as patrolmen and precinct captain.

Given their dependence on political connections to hold their jobs, it is not surprising that officers remained responsive to the needs of district politicos, even to the point of turning out the vote in local elections for the party that employed them. Since they were political rather than merit employees, the old practice of appointing physically unfit officers, so reminiscent of the nightwatch system, was continued in the early days of the new police. The police were still not free to enforce laws that popular majorities or politically powerful groups did not want enforced, nor could they overlook offenses that the party in power or public opinion wanted suppressed. Thus in cities controlled by Whigs or American Republicans, the police were expected to enforce the Sunday closing, licensing, and ten-gallon laws; in Democratically controlled areas, a police officer could expect to be looking for a job if he tried to enforce any of those statutes.

The American police were further unlike their English counterparts in that they were caught in the middle of the ethnic tensions and battles that were dividing pre-Civil War American cities. The Philadelphia and New York police, when under American Republican mayors, spent much of their time battling Irish and Democratic gangs and fire companies. There is some indication that these administrations recruited nativist gang members and fire b'hoys to serve as police officers, thereby instantly converting what had been ethnic street wars into struggles to uphold "law and order." Under Democratic Mayor Richard Vaux, who served from 1856 to 1858, Philadelphia saw a rapid decline in the rate of gang and firemen's fights, mostly because the police were composed nonpartisanly of some of the city's toughest Irish and native street fighters. Paid to search out gangs and thugs as part of their preventive strategy, "Dick Vaux's Police" developed a fearsome reputation in the late 1850s for brass-knuckle policing. The Philadelphia Police Department's official historian described the mayor's tactics in handling the notorious Schulkill Rangers, a gang that for years had terrorized Moyamensing:

> There was no formal arrest, there were few prisoners in the dock
> in the mornings; the justices of the peace were not much troubled,
> but the fellow who was caught never forgot until his dying day the

time he fell into the hands of Dick Vaux's police. I remember one night three of the Rangers were surprised, and jumped into the river and swam to a tug-boat in the middle of the stream. It was very cold, and they thought that Dick (I was there) and his men would not follow. They were never so mistaken in all their lives. We got a boat and overtook them. The interview was more muscular than intellectual. The rascals were pretty well satisfied before it was over. So were we. They didn't trouble us again during the administration.[1]

Thanks to police tactics such as these, Philadelphia, New York, and the major cities of the Northeast were far less violent on the eve of the Civil War than they had been in the preceding two decades. No innovation or reform before or since has done as much to alter the quality of life in American cities.

1. Quoted in Sam Bass Warner, Jr., *The Private City: Philadelphia in Three Periods of Its Growth* (Philadelphia, 1968), p. 97.

# 7. Jacksonian Violence
## in Historical Perspective

By itself, improved policing cannot fully account for the decline in urban violence that characterized the 1850s. Of the many other factors that contributed to the increasing tranquility of the pre-Civil War decade, the most obvious one was the growing acceptance of the abolition movement. While anti-abolitionist mobs were rarely as disruptive or threatening as racial or ethnic rioters, they did cause the largest number of collective disorders in the decade of the 1830s. But even ethnic rioting, perhaps the most virulent and angry form of Jacksonian collective violence, declined somewhat after the 1840s, thus adding to the growing calm. By the 1850s, it would appear, municipal politics had absorbed much of the energies that nativist and immigrants had been investing in street violence. Local politics could provide an alternative battleground because, in the long run, the issues over which the two sides were fighting were capable of being resolved through the electoral process. Control of local school boards and control of local police departments could determine how a community would regulate its liquor consumption, how it would keep the peace on the Sabbath, whether it would permit sporting events, gambling, and other activities that offended evangelicals, and whether the Bible would be used as a reading text in the community's public schools. Nativists in Philadelphia, New York, Boston, Baltimore, and New Orleans worked energetically on ward and district levels to elect their own true believers to public office. In Philadelphia, for example, the American Republican party was able to elect two representatives to Congress in 1844, and one of them, Lewis C. Levin, managed to win reelection to a second term. By 1848, the last vestiges of Philadelphia American Republican electoral strength on the county and state level were gone, but in Kensington, Southwark, and Moyamensing, where large pockets of committed nativists resided, the American Republicans were able to maintain control of district commissionerships, school boards, constables' offices, and the night watch. Their grip of local law enforcement and school policy in these districts was not broken until 1854, when the state legislature consolidated the city and county of Philadelphia into a single jurisdiction and abolished the district governments.

There were at least two serendipitous factors that helped further reduce violent confrontations between nativists and Irish immigrants in Jacksonian cities. One was the return of confidence that accompanied the economic upswing of the post-1844 period. Another was the outbreak, in 1846, of the war with Mexico. The war helped reduce riots in American cities by drawing away more than 100,000 young soldiers, many of whom had been combatants in gang and fire fights. Perhaps just as important, the war against Mexico was a war against a Catholic power, and at its outset there was some question of whether the immigrant Irish would fight for their adopted homeland against their fellow Catholics. But the Irish soldiers generally proved as anti-

Mexican as their native-born Protestant counterparts. Thousands of Irish volunteers fought valiantly in Texas and Mexico, and the nation paid tribute to those immigrants who gave their lives to insure Texas's secession from Mexico and its annexation to the United States.

Anti-immigrant sentiments, however, did not disappear from American politics in the 1850s. In the early part of the decade, the old American Republican organizations reappeared in urban centers as the American, or Know-Nothing, party, which gained some state-wide electoral successes in Pennsylvania, New York, Massachusetts, and Louisiana. One sign of nativism's presence in the late 1850s was the creation by a Know-Nothing legislature of the Massachusetts State Police, the nation's first state police department. These police officers did not patrol highways and rural areas as state police forces do today; instead, they enforced the state's prohibition laws in Boston, where a Democratic city government refused to do so. Know-Nothingism, like American Republicanism, never generated the national support it would have needed to change the naturalization laws and other federal controls over immigration. When nativism finally attained national power, it did so only by merging with the growing Free Soil movement to form the Republican party, which ran its first presidential candidate in 1856 and which elected Abraham Lincoln to the White House in 1860. By then, the immigrant issue had taken a back seat to the secession issue.

Just as political nativism did not completely disappear in the years after the violent 1840s, neither did ethnic rioting. In 1871, New Yorkers were stunned by the massive Orange Riots, in which a Protestant Irish parade provoked Irish Catholic hecklers to fight and throw rocks, which in turn provoked militiamen to open fire and kill a hundred combatants and onlookers. Anti-Chinese rioting in California took the lives of Chinese immigrants in the 1870s and 1880s, and in 1891 a New Orleans mob lynched eleven Italian immigrants. Yet the frequency and intensity of ethnic rioting never reached the heights it had attained in the turbulent era of the 1830s and 1840s.

While the 1850s seem to have marked a turning point in the history of American collective violence, it would be inaccurate to say that characteristically Jacksonian forms of rioting did not recur after the Civil War. Until the 1940s, for example, race riots continued to be characterized by whites invading black communities and inflicting destruction and death on black residents. Vigilante groups in the West and Southwest still continued to apply summary justice to thieves, murderers, and moral offenders, while southern lynch mobs used intimidation and murder to drive blacks and Carpetbaggers out of local politics during the era of Reconstruction.

In one major respect, however, post-Civil War collective violence differed radically from its Jacksonian forerunner: The major form that rioting took in the years after 1877 was labor and industrial violence. The United States emerged from the war with a full-fledged industrial system in which workers found themselves toiling under oppressive and dangerous conditions in massive factories, on railroads, in steel mills and coal mines, and in confining sweat shops and retail shops. Wages generally were kept low, and the large majority of employers refused to permit workers to organize unions or strike for better wages and working conditions. As the battle for workers' rights and especially the right to unionize led to strikes and violent confrontations between labor and management, the nation's middle classes and law enforcement officials girded themselves for the prospect of class warfare.

While workers had such weapons as strikes, attacks on strikebreakers, sabotage, destruction of plants and equipment, assassination, and general rioting in their arsenals, most American industrial violence in the late nineteenth and early twentieth centuries was not a fair fight between workers and employers. Major capitalists such as John D. Rockefeller and Andrew Carnegie spent freely to hire well-armed private police forces such as the Pinkertons to protect their property and scab employees. Strikers and union organizers bitterly resented these hired vigilantes and fought several pitched battles against them, most notably during the 1892 strike at Carnegie Steel's Homestead plant outside Pittsburgh, when both strikers and Pinkertons were killed in an exchange of gunfire.

Shrewd employers not only hired private guards but also cultivated relationships with state militia commanders, governors, chiefs of police, and mayors, and were thus often able to call on public law enforcement officials during labor disputes. Capitalists contributed heavily to the cost of building state militia armories in center city areas, so that militia units could be gathered quickly with their equipment and arms in the event of industrial or urban unrest. State militia and federal troops were centrally involved in suppressing many major labor disputes of the late nineteenth and early twentieth centuries: the 1886 Haymarket riot; the Pullman strike and national railroad strikes of 1894; the Colorado silver mining strikes of the 1890s and early 1900s; and the Pennsylvania anthracite strikes of the 1900s among others.

Local police departments often proved reliable allies of management in local labor disputes. Their strategy of preventive patrol meant that the police were almost always on hand when striking workers were picketing a factory or other establishment. The creation of police barracks and the invention of the police telegraph in the late 1880s meant that officers in the field could summon large numbers of reinforcements on short notice if strikes grew disorderly, or if strikers forcibly attempted to keep scab workers from crossing their picket lines. The local police were generally expected to keep order, and under growing pressure from major industrialists, local police departments increasingly defined this role to mean that they were defenders of industrial property and the right of scabs to work where and when they chose. Although there were some cases in smaller cities when the local police refused to use force against strikers and even, in the name of public order, compelled scabs to board trains and leave town, the police in metropolitan industrial centers such as Cleveland, Chicago, Pittsburgh, and Buffalo lined up solidly with employers during labor disputes. As the history of industrial violence illustrates, after the Civil War the relatively even balance of power between rioters and peace-keeping forces that had characterized the Jacksonian period had shifted decisively in favor of the authorities.

If, in fact, many forms of Jacksonian violence were no longer common in post-Civil War America; if private groups no longer clashed in firemen's fights, anti-abolition riots, or election riots; if police departments took over the job of urban peacekeeping from the inefficient and politically limited constabulary and night watch, can it be said that there is some historical legacy of Jacksonian violence that can help us understand the history of violence in later periods? Is there any historical continuity between pre- and post-Civil War violence, and is there any way to describe the influence of Jacksonian violence on the forms of violence that have succeeded it?

As with most speculation about historical causation or influence, it is possible to argue contradictory positions about the same set of facts. For example, one might argue that Jacksonian violence had an impact on both northern and southern willingness to fight the Civil War. Their frequent exposure to Jacksonian fighting and bloodshed might have immunized northern urbanites against believing that violence is avoidable or exceptional in human affairs. Northerners might thus have found the prospect of resisting southern secession by force of arms a less than radical prospect; the success of northern city govern-ments in suppressing riots by means of police departments might have encouraged northerners to support a parallel military response to southern "lawlessness." On the other hand, southerners might well have interpreted collective violence, social disorganization, and ethnic and racial disharmony in the North to mean that such a riot-torn society could not muster the resources to resist the South's departure from the Union. Southerners might also have believed that the relative immunity of northern anti-abolition and anti-immigrant mobs indicated racist and pro-slavery sentiment in the North, or that northern state and municipal governments lacked the will and organization to suppress any violent resistance to federal efforts to end slavery in the South. To a degree such an assessment of northern opinion was accurate. In 1863, when President Lincoln announced the emancipation of southern slaves and soon after established a system of conscription into the Union army, thousands of potential draftees in New York and Boston rose up in rebellion, and it took the full effort of the New York Police Department and several detachments of federal troops to quell the rioting in New York. It seems unlikely that the New York Draft Riots of 1863, in and of themselves, could have crippled the Union war effort, but had the forces of order been less successful in suppressing the uprising, northern morale might well have suffered a severe blow.

Such speculation about the effects of Jacksonian collective violence on the history of the Civil War are enlightening for the historian and, I hope, suggestive for the reader, but they should be understood as conditional guesses rather than historical truths. Whatever lessons we may take from our study of Jacksonian rioting, it seems important above all to recognize the degree to which collective violence was integrated into the political and social processes of Jacksonian society. Indeed, for competing groups or persons who believed strongly in their political opinions or cultural outlook, violence was an always available and frequently resorted to option for dealing with rivals or with local government. To a greater degree than today, riot played an integral part in intergroup relations and local politics. In the absence of a preventive police force or a strong military establishment, disaffected, mobilized, and committed groups in Jacksonian America were *relatively* free to express their dominance, test their opponents' strength, or express their unhappiness by means of force. Nowhere is this more true than in the case of anti-abolition and anti-black rioting, since there were few defenders of either abolitionists or blacks in the 1830s and 1840s. But the same was true for anti-Mormons and nativists, even though Mormons and immigrants, especially the Irish, were in a better position to defend themselves.

Political scientist H. L. Neiburg has formulated an explanation for collective violence in the 1960s that applies equally well to the experience of the 1830s and 1840s:

> Extreme and violent political behavior cannot be dismissed as erratic, exceptional, and meaningless. To set it apart from the processes that are characteristic of society is to ignore the continuum that exists between peaceable and disruptive behavior; it is to deny the role of violence in creating and testing political legitimacy and in conditioning the terms of all social bargaining and adjustment. Violence in all forms, up to and including assassination, is a natural form of political behavior.[1]

Neiburg concludes, in words that could be applied directly to the Jacksonian mobs who tarred and feathered abolitionists, who burned Catholic churches, who shot and killed Mormons, or who lynched and beat blacks, that "the threat of violence—pure pain and damage—can be used to coerce and to deter, to intimidate and to blackmail, to demoralize and to paralyze, purposefully and meaningfully in a process of social bargaining."[2]

This is not to say that collective violence is "normal" or "natural" in the sense of "acceptable" or even "excusable." Neiburg is not recommending that violence become a respected part of our national politics. He is saying, however, that violence has been an *integral* part, no matter how shabby, of the nation's history and of its contemporary politics. Under most conditions, power, wealth, and status get distributed to various groups in society through peaceful interactions such as the passage of laws, bargaining in the marketplace, electoral campaigns, legal inheritance, the educational system, and the attribution of prestige in the media. At other times, groups have sought to control the distribution of power or rewards through strikes, riots, demonstrations, and collective uprisings. Neiburg is warning us that it

---

1. H. L. Neiburg, *Political Violence* (New York, 1969), p. 5.
2. Neiburg, p. 6.

would be incorrect to think of the first, more peaceful set of processes as "normal" and the second, more violent or coercive set of tactics as "aberrational," "abnormal," "immoral," or "un-American." It is probably going too far to call collective violence "as American as cherry pie;" after all, Americans neither invented rioting nor hold a monopoly on its use. Instead, collective violence should be understood historically as one of a number of methods that private groups and governments have used to fix the terms under which they have settled their conflicts.

The history of Jacksonian violence shows that, for the most part, private groups have used collective violence in one of two ways: as part of their political relationship to other groups, or as a means for expressing their beliefs, emotions, or recreational needs. In the political realm most Jacksonian violence was preservatist in intent. It is obvious that, in the long run, violence could not serve indefinitely to maintain the Jacksonian status quo: Despite the nativist destruction of Kensington, for example, Irish immigrants kept flooding into American ports; the assassination of Joseph and Hyrum Smith did not prevent the Mormon church from gathering converts to its religious communities; the murder of Elijah Lovejoy neither silenced the abolition movement nor prevented the emancipation of the slaves. But as a tactic for closing Lovejoy's press, or as a method for driving the Mormons out of Illinois, or as a way to discourage Irish immigrants from settling in Philadelphia, such riots proved immediately effective.

By many measures American cities are far more peaceable and secure today than they were in the 1830s and 1840s. The number of Americans killed or injured in collective violence in the 1970s is far smaller than it was in the 1840s, even though the nation's current population is many times greater than it was in that earlier period. Local, state, and national governments have armed themselves heavily since the 1960s to deal forcefully with rioters. If governments choose *not* to crush disorders with overwhelming force—as the New York Police Department chose not to do during the great Blackout of

1977—they do so for political or humanitarian reasons, not because they lack the capacity to suppress riots. Yet if history has any predictive power, and if Neiburg's observations are of any value, we can expect to experience various forms of collective violence—both familiar and new—at some time in the nation's foreseeable future. So long as groups continue to conflict, and so long as violence remains a part of the nation's political processes, rioting and the attempt to suppress it will once again fill the nation's streets with violence, destruction, and, regrettably, death.

# Bibliographical Essay

The body of historical studies of American collective violence has grown considerably since the uprisings and riots of the 1960s stimulated interest in the roots of American disorder. It is fair to say, however, that violence in the Jacksonian era has not been overly studied. The works listed below represent the best of the available volumes on violence in American history in general and during the Jacksonian years specifically. I have omitted the titles of scholarly articles because of their relative inaccessibility to those not on college campuses. Readers interested in relevant articles are referred to the footnotes of this work and, for a very thorough accounting, to the footnotes of Richard Maxwell Brown's, "Patterns of American Violence," in his excellent *Strain of Violence: Historical Studies of American Violence and Vigilantism* (New York, 1975). Other general works on the history of American violence that devote attention to the Jacksonian era include: Hugh Davis Graham and Ted Robert Gurr, *The History of Violence in America* (New York, 1969); Richard Maxwell Brown, ed., *American Violence* (Englewood Cliffs, N.J., 1970); Richard Hofstadter and Michael Wallace, eds., *American Violence: A Documentary History* (New York, 1970); and Thomas Rose, ed., *Violence in America: A Historical and Contemporary Reader* (New York, 1970).

Most of the major riots described in this work have been studied elsewhere at greater length. For the history of collective violence in pre-Civil War Philadelphia, see Sam Bass Warner, Jr., *The Private City: Philadelphia in Three Periods of Its Growth* (Philadelphia, 1968), particularly chapter 7. The Native American Riots of 1844 are more fully explored in Michael Feldberg, *The Philadelphia Riots of 1844: A Study of Ethnic Conflict* (Westport, Conn., 1975). Other cities also have received attention. For New York, see James F. Richardson, *The New York Police: Colonial Times to 1901* (New York, 1970); Herbert Asbury, *The Gangs of New York: An Informal History of the Underworld* (New York, 1928); Adrian Cook, *The Armies of the Streets: The New York Draft Riots of 1863* (Lexington, Mass., 1974); and Joel Tyler Headley, *The Great Riots of New York, 1712 to 1873* (New York, 1873). For Boston, see Roger Lane, *Policing the City: Boston, 1822-1885* (Cambridge, Mass., 1967).

Anti-abolition rioting has received attention from various historians, but none has studied the phenomenon more closely or intelligently than Leonard L. Richards in his *"Gentlemen of Property and Standing": Anti-Abolition Mobs in Jacksonian America* (New York, 1970). Nativist violence in cities other than Philadelphia receives some attention in Ray A. Billington, *The Protestant Crusade, 1800-1860: A Study of the Origins of American Nativism* (New York, 1938). Racial violence in the North is touched on by Leon F. Litwack, *North of Slavery: The Negro in the Free States, 1790-1860* (Chicago, 1961). For racial violence in the South see Arthur F. Raper, *The*

*Tragedy of Lynching* (Chapel Hill, 1938) and William Styron's fictional account, *The Confessions of Nat Turner* (New York, 1966). Anti-Mormon violence is treated in Dallin H. Oaks and Marvin S. Hill, *Carthage Conspiracy: The Trial of the Accused Assassins of Joseph Smith* (Urbana, Ill., 1975). Of the numerous studies of violence against the various tribes and peoples who make up the American Indians, a useful place to start is William T. Hagen, *American Indians* (Chicago, 1961).

# Index